Fare Stage Series
Volume Five

TODMORDEN BUSES
A CENTURY OF SERVICE

Ralph Wilkinson

Nostalgia Road Publications

Contents

The **Nostalgia Road** Series ™

is produced under licence by

Nostalgia Road Publications Ltd.
Units 5 - 8, Chancel Place, Shap Road Industrial Estate,
Kendal, Cumbria, LA9 6NZ
Tel. +44 (0)1539 738832 - Fax: +44 (0)1539 730075

designed and published by
Trans-Pennine Publishing Ltd.
PO Box 10, Appleby-in-Westmorland, Cumbria, CA16 6FA
Tel. +44 (0)17683 51053 Fax. +44 (0)17683 53558
e-mail: admin@transpenninepublishing.co.uk

and printed by
Kent Valley Colour Printers Ltd.
Kendal, Cumbria - +44 (0)1539 741344

Front Cover: *In the late 1950s, a 1951 Leyland PD2/12 No. 20 climbs past Ormerod Taylor & Sons Ltd's factory between Walsden and Lanebottom. It is pursued by a Leyland 'White Lady' operating the Ribble X4 Burnley-Manchester service, a scene which could be observed at approx. 20 minutes past each odd hour.*
From an original painting commissioned by author from the late G S Cooper

Rear Cover Top: *Against the well-known backdrop of the town centre railway viaduct, a 1950 Leyland PD2/1 JWY 824 displays its new Calderdale JOC. number 352 with its older Todmorden livery as it waits at the Cross Lee starting point in Burnley Road, Todmorden in 1971.* **Photobus**

Rear Cover Bottom: *A 1969 dual purpose Leyland PSU4A/4R Fleet No. 8 (BWU 689H) with Pennine bodywork is seen here in its private hire role on loan to Ribble.*
Seddon Archive

Title Page: *With St Mary's Church in the background, PD2/1 No. 1 (GWU 11) crosses from Church Street (Rochdale Road) to North Street (Burnley Road) in Todmorden town centre. The author's mother was the first fare-paying passenger to travel on this bus in February 1948.* **John Fozard**

This Page: *Leyland 'X' No. 8 (B5628) was photographed on the present-day A681 at Rams Lumb, near Cloughfoot, on 2nd August 1913, two days after its arrival in Todmorden. Its chassis was one of two Todmorden bus chassis to be impressed by the Home Office for war duties in 1914.* **TAS**

ISBN 1 903016 68 1
British Cataloguing in Publication Data
A catalogue record for this book is available from the British Library

INTRODUCTION

Above: *L1 No.37 (573 EYG), which joined the fleet new in January 1964, is seen in Smith Street, Rochdale, on the Saturdays only Limited Stop service operated jointly with Rochdale Corporation Transport. This bus, operating the same service is the subject of an EFE model (see page 28).* Photobus

New Year's Day 2007 marks the centenary of Todmorden's pioneering motor omnibus service. Eastbourne was the first local authority in the British Isles to have operated motor buses exclusively; Todmorden was the second.The town of Todmorden lies in Yorkshire's Calder Valley deep in the heart of the South Pennines. The infant River Calder, flowing from the north-west through the upper part of the valley, known locally as the Burnley Valley, is joined in the town centre by the Walsden Water, which runs from the south through the locally-named Rochdale Valley. From the confluence of these two streams, the enlarged River Calder flows in a roughly easterly direction towards Halifax. A fourth, even narrower, defile, the Bacup Valley, joins the Rochdale Valley from the west about 3/4 mile south of the town centre.

Until 1st January 1888, the Lancashire/Yorkshire border ran through the centre of the town, where it was straddled by the Town Hall. Moving the county boundary on that date to bring the whole town within the West Riding of Yorkshire no doubt facilitated the incorporation of the Borough of Todmorden in 1896. Since 1st April 1974, Todmorden has formed part of the Calderdale Metropolitan Borough in the administrative county of West Yorkshire.

Writing this brief history has been an exercise of unashamed nostalgia for me. I have deliberately tried to keep technical jargon to a minimum, while trying to maintain the interest of transport enthusiasts. My aim has been to re-create something of the 'atmosphere' of the service operated by Todmorden's Brunswick green and cream buses, which are still remembered with pride and affection by many Todmordians worldwide.

Ralph Wilkinson Grange over Sands November 2006

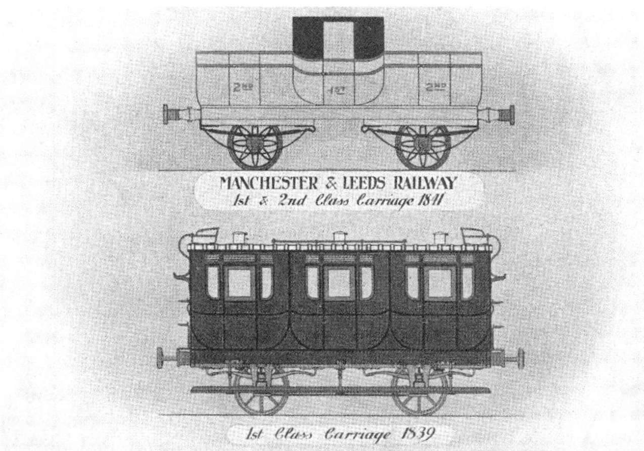

THE BACKGROUND SCENE

Following an Act of 1760, turnpike roads were constructed from Halifax to Todmorden and thence to Burnley and to Littleborough, where the earlier Halifax to Rochdale via Ripponden turnpike was joined. These largely superseded the ancient packhorse tracks and expedited the development of housing and industry away from the hills and along the valley floors. Construction of the trans-Pennine Rochdale Canal through Todmorden was completed in 1804. This enabled much larger quantities of goods to be carried more efficiently and at less cost than hitherto and played a vital part in the development of the cotton industry in the town. In 1821 a horse-drawn coach service commenced, calling at the *Golden Lion* Inn, Todmorden, where the four horses were regularly changed and where an early post office was established. The two coaches used, the *Perseverance* and the *Shuttle*, carried letters as well as passengers.

The Summit Gap, between Littleborough and Todmorden, attracted the attention of early railway promoters as the easiest route across the South Pennines. An 1831 Parliamentary Bill was defeated because of opposition from the canal company, but five years later an Act was passed for the Manchester & Leeds Railway, which was to become the main line of the Lancashire & Yorkshire Railway (L&YR) With George Stephenson as its engineer, it was completed in March 1841. A branch from Todmorden to Burnley was opened as a single line in 1849, being doubled to meet demand in 1860. A short connecting line from Hall Royd to Stansfield Hall was built in 1862, enabling trains travelling from Hebden Bridge to Burnley to do so without reversing at Todmorden. This resulted in many trains by-passing Todmorden station, a situation which was only partly remedied by the opening of an additional passenger station at the less central location of Stansfield Hall in 1869.

Top Left: *Wide boat* Mary Ann, *with family/crew, on the Rochdale Canal near Kilnhurst bridge, Todmorden, c1890.*
The Jack Uttley Photo Library

Middle Left: *Imagine travelling second-class in a state-of-the-art M&LR carriage in 1841 through the newly opened Summit Tunnel, then the longest in the world, behind a struggling steam locomotive!* L&YR

Bottom Left: *A Todmorden & District Carriage Company's horse-bus approaches the town centre along Burnley Road near the foot of Ferney Lee Road at Toad Carr.*
Todmorden Antiquarian Society (TAS)

26 ADVERTISEMENT.

Todmorden & District Carriage Co.,

LIMITED,

LIVERY STABLES.

PAVEMENT, TODMORDEN.

Wish to direct the attention of the public to their new premises at Pavement, adjoining the old Coaching House, "The Golden Lion Inn." Having obtained the premises lately occupied by the Canal Company, and having erected thereon commodious Stables, Coach Houses, &c. They are prepared to supply every description of vehicles for the convenience and comfort of the public; **FOUR-IN-HAND, TANDEM TURNOUTS, OMNIBUSSES, WAGGONETTES, DRAGS, CABS,** in first-class style. Picnic, Wedding, Excursionist, and all other Parties, attended to with punctuality and despatch.

MOURNING DEPARTMENT.—Hearses, Mourning Coaches, and Funeral 'Busses supplied on the shortest notice, and with the greatest care.

They are also prepared to supply orders for Hay, Straw, Corn, &c., in large or small quantities.

Attendance at the office, on the premises, daily, from 7 a.m. to 10 p.m.

Above: *From the Todmorden & Hebden Bridge Historical Almanack for 1882.*

Even with six railway stations within the town - Todmorden, Walsden, Eastwood, Stansfield Hall, Cornholme and Portsmouth - there was a demand for convenient local road transport and a number of enterprising carriage proprietors established themselves as private hire cab operators. In 1875, the Todmorden & District Carriage Company Limited was established on the initiative of Mr Jonathan Gledhill. On 10th April, the company began operating a local bus service on Saturday afternoons and evenings from the town centre along the Burnley valley to the toll bar at Cornholme, using horse buses previously owned by John Ormerod, who had recently retired from his business of 'Omnibus and Cab Proprietor and Funeral Undertaker'. Six months later, a second Saturday service, via Halifax Road to the Woodman Inn at Charlestown, was commenced. This was subsequently extended to Hebden Bridge and a service to the *Waggon & Horses Inn* at Walsden was established. All the company's services were developed to operate six days per week, facilitated by the expiry of the Todmorden Turnpike Trust on 31st October 1878.

The need for convenient local passenger transport systems was met in nearby urban areas by the construction of tramways, mostly by private companies, following the 1870 Tramways Act.

Some tramways were initially horse-drawn systems, whilst others were steam-powered when built, but all were later municipalised and electrified. In 1905, Rochdale extended its system to Summit, within a mile of the Todmorden borough boundary, but the nearest Burnley's trams came was a local line to Towneley, opened in 1904. An extensive network of tramways, extending from Accrington to Bacup, five miles west of Todmorden, was developed in the Rossendale valley. Halifax opened a line as far as Hebden Bridge centre in 1902 and in July of that year a new Bill sanctioned an extension to the Todmorden boundary at Sandbed, though this was never constructed.

At the 1901 census, the population of Todmorden was over 25,000, a level which was to be maintained throughout the next decade. In that year, the Borough Council employed a firm of consultants to advise on electric lighting, power and tramways. The advisers recommended that new electricity works be built at Millwood - (these opened on 13th October 1905) - and that a tramshed be sited in close proximity.

Top Left: *Burnley Corporation Tramways electric tramcar No. 4 is seen operating the Rosegrove service, which opened in July 1903, in St. James's Street, Burnley. The 71-seater Milnes car was one of 24 built in 1901 for the electrification and conversion to the four feet gauge of the Burnley system.* Pamlin Prints

Middle Left: *Rochdale Corporation Tramways' line to Littleborough was converted to the standard gauge of 4' $8^{1}/_{2}$", electrified and extended to the* Summit Inn *in 1905. Brush car No.19, dating from 1903, is seen at the terminus during the inaugural run on 10th August 1905. The postcard recording this scene was posted to one of the author's relatives three days later.*

Bottom Left: *Halifax Corporation Tramways Brush car No.73, dating from 1902, is seen at the New Road terminus, Hebden Bridge, c1910. The system operated on the narrow gauge of 3' 6", originally approved by Parliament in 1883 for a cable tramway that was never built.*
The Alice Longstaff Gallery Collection

A single line tramway was proposed along each of Todmorden's three main valleys, with double-track loops every half-mile to allow cars travelling in opposite directions to pass. Allowing for a five-minute interval service along the Burnley Valley and a 12-minute headway along the other routes, the estimated cost of the track, cables, overhead equipment and tramcars was £71,110. Following a successful application to the Board of Trade, 'The Todmorden Corporation Tramways Order' of 1902 authorised the construction of tramways within the Borough, but the Corporation was slow to take further action, mainly for financial reasons.

A small number of private carriers and waggonette owners began to experiment with motor-buses. These included Ezra Laycock of Cowling, between Keighley and Colne, who is generally credited with running the first motor bus service in Yorkshire. A few municipalities, including Southampton and Manchester, also trialled motor buses, but most of these were quickly abandoned in favour of their more reliable trams. Todmorden Council's officers concluded that where a tramway infrastructure already existed, the economics of running passenger vehicles worked out in favour of trams rather than buses. Where it did not, buses were an option worthy of consideration, as no major capital costs, other than the vehicles themselves, were involved.

The Council's Finance & General Purposes Committee (F&GPC) set up a cross-party 'Motor Sub-Committee', comprising Alderman Ashworth and Councillors Dawson, Handley, Jackson and Wilkinson. This held its first meeting on 15th August 1905, when Coun. James Wilkinson was elected Chairman.

At its second meeting, the sub-committee decided to visit Coun. Wilkinson's home town of Colne to see the Laycock & Stephenson bus and "to make enquiries". This was followed by a visit by four of the sub-committee to London, Eastbourne and Birmingham at a cost of £6. 7s. 10d each. Though some members had reservations about the reliability and power of the new and virtually untested mode of transport, a special meeting of the F&GPC held on 1st November 1905 resolved "to promote a Bill in the next Session of Parliament for the establishment of a service of motor 'busses (sic) for this Borough...." It was agreed that the vacant space in the boiler house of the new electricity works be adapted as a temporary bus garage.

A public meeting was held in Todmorden Town Hall on 11th January 1906, at which the Mayor stated that it was proposed to purchase and run motor buses from the Town Hall to Summit, Hebden Bridge, Towneley and Bacup, thus connecting with each of the neighbouring tram systems. A Mr Shaw of Rose Bank suggested that if the Corporation could not see their way to establishing electric tramways they should let someone else come in and do it.

Above: *For his first motor-bus adventure, Ezra Laycock of Cowling entered into partnership with W. Stephenson of Skipton. In 1905 the firm ordered a Milnes-Daimler single-decker to operate a service between Kildwick and Laneshawbridge, the easterly limit of Colne's tram system. AK 335, known locally as* The Monster*, was inspected by members of Todmorden Corporation's Motor Sub-Committee later that year. Stephenson left the partnership in 1912, but Ezra Laycock Ltd. continued trading until 1972, when the company was taken over by Pennine of Gargrave.* Keighley News

Coun. Wilkinson staunchly defended the proposals, conjecturing that it was "a matter for the future to decide whether the motor bus will not displace the tramways in other towns". His arguments must have been convincing, for when the resolution was put to the meeting, it was carried unanimously. However, the subsequent Todmorden Corporation Act, 1906, like the earlier Tramway's order, only allowed the Corporation to operate services *within* the Borough.

MOTOR BUS PIONEERS

In April 1906, the Motor Sub-Committee became the Motor Buses Committee (MBC). Quotes were invited from three companies, following which two 40hp chassis were ordered from the Critchley-Norris Motor Company of Bamber Bridge and two 50hp chassis (though such a powerful model had not hitherto been made) from the Lancashire Steam Motor Company Limited of Leyland. Both these manufacturers had strong connections with the pioneering Crossley Brothers of Manchester. Electrically-lit bodies, accommodating 16 passengers on two longitudinal seats in the lower deck, tramcar-style, and 18 passengers on six rows of forward-facing seats on the open-air upper deck, were ordered for all four from the United Electric Car Company Ltd. tram builders, of Preston. Before the year-end, the MBC had appointed a foreman driver, Mr J. Stevenson, six other drivers and six conductors from a large number of applicants, though one wonders how many of the drivers had any actual experience of driving!

Above: *The 1906 Critchley-Norris at Todmorden Town Hall about to embark on the historic first journey to Steanor Bottom on New Year's Day 1907. The Mayor, Ald. Abraham Crossley (in hat and long coat) is on the right of the picture. The bus, which carried its maker's temporary registration number 'B1P' - its permanent registration was C 1503 - became Fleet No.2, though the decision to number the buses was not taken until 16th January 1907 and the numbers did not appear on the vehicles until later.* TAS

Uniforms were bought and ancillary equipment was either purchased or hired and arrangements were made for advertising on the buses. It was agreed that the service should operate on every day of the week (albeit with a reduced service on Sundays) and that the first bus should start from the Town Hall at 10.00 am on New Year's Day 1907. Early on Saturday 29th December 1906 a deputation, including the Mayor and Coun. Wilkinson, went to Bamber Bridge to collect the two Critchley-Norris vehicles and were accompanied on the return journey by Mr. Norris and two of his employees.

Top Right: *This picture of No.2, with a group of excited boys at Black Rock, Cornholme, is dated 31st December 1906, suggesting that it was taken during a trial run on the day before the official first journey. Despite its destination blind, it was not on a marathon journey to the south coast!* TAS

Middle Right: *Critchley had worked for Crossley Bros. before forming 'The Critchley-Norris Motor Company' with Norris of Peter Pilkington Limited. Lancashire Steam (which later became Leyland) also used Crossley engines in their early petrol-driven vehicles.* TAS

Bottom Right: *An early 1907 picture of the second Critchley-Norris. Registered C 1504, it became, somewhat illogically, No.1! It is seen here at Lanebottom, between Walsden and Summit with Driver (his cap badge reads Motorman) William Nothard and Conductor Miles Craven. Nos. 1 and 2 appear to have shared the temporary registration number 'B1P'.* *See page 32 for a view taken at this location 50-years later.* TAS

After an adventurous journey in wintry conditions, the party returned home at 7.30pm in one of the two new buses, driven by Mr Stevenson. The second one 'froze-up' at Burnley en-route, but arrived in Todmorden later in the evening, having been revived by the Critchley-Norris men.

The MBC met on New Year's Eve and, considering the heavy snowfalls of the previous few days, agreed the postponement of the eagerly-awaited new bus service. Fortunately, in view of the scepticism that was spreading among some of the townspeople, a thaw set in and by noon it had begun to rain. A hastily convened meeting of councillors agreed that the service could begin with a run along the Rochdale valley. Shortly after 2.00pm, bus No.2 began to load, first with councillors, then with local citizens from the crowd. Many had to be turned away disappointed, as did more along the route. For this historic first run by a Todmorden bus, the driver was Tom Suthers and the conductor was Albert Steel. Also on board were Mr Stevenson and one of the Critchley-Norris employees.

As the bus moved slowly away on its bumpy journey, the crowd broke into spontaneous applause. Beyond the first mile at Copperashouse, the condition of the road deteriorated and beyond the second mile at Walsden Waggon, it became no more than a snow-lined track. Nevertheless, within 25 minutes the vehicle arrived at Steanor Bottom, just over three miles from the town centre, where it reversed into Calderbrook Road and returned. As the *Todmorden & Hebden Bridge Historical Almanack* for 1908 recorded: "although the roads were in shocking condition owing to the thaw, an excellent run was made".

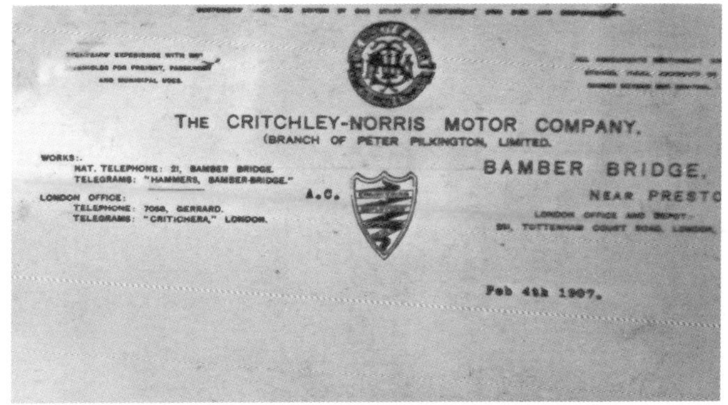

THE CRITCHLEY-NORRIS MOTOR COMPANY.
(BRANCH OF PETER PILKINGTON, LIMITED.

WORKS:.
NAT. TELEPHONE: 21, BAMBER BRIDGE.
TELEGRAMS: "HAMMERS, BAMBER-BRIDGE."

LONDON OFFICE:
TELEPHONE: 7058, GERRARD.
TELEGRAMS: "CRITICHERA," LONDON.

A.C.

BAMBER BRIDGE,
NEAR PRESTO

Feb 4th 1907.

Top Left: *Todmorden's first Lancashire Steam bus was this 1907 Model 'U'. It became Fleet No.3 (B 2079).*
Roy Marshall Collection/Leyland

Middle Left: *By the end of February 1907, the fleet had increased in number to four. No.4, seen here at Sandbed, was identical to No.3. The driver is F W Bjorling, from Sweden, known widely and affectionately as 'Von Tromp'.* TAS

Bottom Left: *Staff, passengers and a dog pose for the camera in this further view of No.4, now with its registration plate B 2082, as it stands near Eastwood Station.*
Roy Marshall Collection/Dennis O'Neill

"Normal" services began on 2nd January 1907. One bus made regular journeys along the Rochdale Valley and the other along the Burnley Valley. Bus stops were indicated by two white bands painted on gas lamp posts, just below the ladder bar, the painter being paid £3 for the whole of his work throughout the borough. Breakdowns, cancellations and even running out of petrol were frequent occurrences, with the result that adherence to the timetable was rare. When one vehicle was out of service for repairs, the other one ran a two-hourly service along each route. During only the second week of operation, the Carriage Company's horse buses had to be recalled into service as both motor buses were under repair! Nevertheless, a contemporary report described the inauguration of the bus service as:-

"... an event of widespread interest and far-reaching importance...... Despite the adverse conditions of the roads, and one or two slight mishaps, the new system of locomotion has excited very favourable comments, and given every satisfaction both to the Motor 'Bus Committee and the public".

A purveyor of 'spin' a century later would have been proud of such a statement!

On 22nd January, the MBC resolved "that when the buses commence running again they each run straight through alternately, in place of one bus for each district as at present". The first of the two motor buses ordered from the Lancashire Steam Company was delivered on the following Saturday and so, with three vehicles available (in theory), a partial service to the borough boundary at Sandbed began on 6th February. Within minutes of the second Lancashire Steam bus arriving three weeks later, it was pressed into service on the Sandbed route!

Fares were calculated at 1d (0.4p) per mile, in overlapping stages, with a minimum fare of one old penny. Thus, for example, a 2 $^{1}/_{2}$ mile journey cost 2 $^{1}/_{2}$ d., but a $^{1}/_{2}$ mile journey cost 1d. Unlike the Carriage Company's fares, no differentiation was made between inside (downstairs) and outside (upstairs) travel.

Above: *With Nos.1 and 2 laid up awaiting spares and No.4 in the garage with a broken crankshaft, the arrival of No.5 (C 1761) on 11th July 1907 immediately doubled the availability of buses for duty! The Burton-on-Trent manufactured Ryknield is seen here at the* Roebuck Inn, *Portsmouth, close to the Lancashire-Yorkshire boundary.* TAS

On 18th March 1907 Mr. J W Hudson was appointed to the post of Traffic Manager at a wage of 30 shillings (£1.50) per week and on the same day, bus No. 2, driven by William Nothard, ran across Halifax Road and into the wall of Roomfield Baptist Chapel after its steering had collapsed. As the year progressed, dissatisfaction among the public increased and the bus service became a standing joke in the town.

During 1907, Lancashire Steam changed its name to Leyland Motors, though, of the buses produced by the company in that year, 36 were steam-powered and only 17 petrol-powered. Numbers. 3 and 4 had engines newly developed in-house by Lancashire Steam fitted into a U-type chassis especially designed by the company for hilly areas, Todmorden being the first customer for this model.

The 50hp. engine ordered by Todmorden proved to be too powerful for (and frequently distorted) some of the component parts, so very few of these engines were produced. Todmorden made further attempts to improve the reliability of its vehicles by the installation of replacement engines from other manufacturers, including Aster (of France) and Belsize.

Above: *The complete fleet, taken in front of the Corporation's gasholder at Millwood in May 1908. From left to right, the buses are Nos. 4, 5, 2, 3 and 1. On 14th April 1908, the Motor Bus Committee authorised the Manager to remove the top-deck seating and stairs of the Ryknield, No.5. However, the bodies of Nos.2 and 5 were interchanged during the process, so it was No.2 that emerged as a single-decker. On 2nd July 1909, No.5 was involved in an accident at Lob Mill, as a result of which its body – originally belonging to No.2 – was substantially destroyed.* TAS

After trialling other makes, including a revolutionary petrol-electric bus powered by a British Thompson Houston engine fitted into a Wolseley-Siddeley chassis, the MBC chose a petrol-engined Ryknield for its fifth vehicle.

When, in November, the time came for the appointment of a Chairman of the Motor Buses Committee for the ensuing year, Coun. Wilkinson refused the nomination. As none of the other members of the Committee were prepared to take on the responsibility and the almost inevitable public odium, the Mayor, Ald. Abraham Crossley, was obliged to assume the Chairmanship. At the January 1908 meeting of the Town Council, Coun. J J Gledhill, son of the secretary of the Carriage Company, proposed that the motor bus service be abandoned as from 31st March 1908, but the motion was adjourned for six months.

During late February 1908, all the buses were off the road and it was not until April that matters began to improve following the return of the buses from their makers after repair. By the time Coun. Gledhill's abandonment resolution was re-considered by the Council at its July meeting, the Mayor was able to report improved reliability and increased takings for the months April-June. The bus service was given a reprieve, though six of the 20 councillors present voted for its abandonment. Coun. Gledhill accepted the decision with good grace and became a staunch supporter of the motor buses.

In 1909, work began on a new bus garage at Millwood. The fleet was increased to seven vehicles by the purchase of two second-hand double-deck motor buses (plus a spare body) from Mr. John Roberts, proprietor of the Rossendale Division Carriage Company, Bacup. One was a 1906 Lancashire-Steam (its original Crossley engine having been replaced by an Aster), which its first Sussex-based owner had unsuccessfully tried to sell to Todmorden shortly after he had bought it. The other, No.7 (B 2064) was a 1907 Critchley-Norris, still with a Crossley engine.

A succession of managers came and went during the early years of the enterprise. In December 1911, a sub-committee of five councillors, together with Mr. Henry Talbot (Gas and Electricity Engineer) and Mr. Gilbert Gill (Bus Manager), visited Leeds and Bradford to inspect the trackless trolley systems in operation in those two cities.

Top Right: *Overlooked by an L&YR locomotive on the railway viaduct, bus No.2, the newly converted single-decker (see previous page), appears to be driving on the 'wrong' side of the road as it passes the* Black Swan *in North Street. Its destination is Springside, then a busy thriving community, $1\frac{1}{2}$ miles from the town centre along the Halifax Valley.* TAS

Middle Right: *Fleet No.6 (AP 2015), a 1906 Lancashire Steam bus purchased second-hand in 1909, decorated for the Coronation of King George V and Queen Mary in 1911. The No.6/AP 2015 combination appeared in several guises up until 1928!*
Roy Marshall Collection/Dennis O'Neill

Bottom Right: *Leyland 'X' No.5 (B 5771), with its wider 'Eastbourne-type' body, cost £715 and became the flagship of the fleet in March 1914. Later that year, its chassis, together with that of No.8 (see page 2), was impressed by the Home Office, never to return.* Leyland Motors

They presented a report, which was enthusiastically in favour of the system being adopted by Todmorden, at the January 1912 meeting of the MBC. Despite the powerful arguments for trolley buses contained in the report, no immediate action appears to have been taken, possibly because a separate Act of Parliament would have been required.

Mr. Gill's report to the September 1912 meeting of the MBC, in which he stated that the throttle control of Bus No.1 had been removed from the dashboard to the steering pillar so as to enable the driver to have better control over the engine, reminds one of the pioneering nature of the undertaking. Major rebuilds of all the vehicles took place between 1912 and 1914, using new Leyland engines and new chassis from Leyland and elsewhere. In addition, a new Leyland 'X' with a second-hand body (No.8) and a completely new Leyland 'X' (No.5, to replace the Ryknield) joined the fleet in August 1913 and March 1914, but within weeks of World War I being declared on 4th August 1914, both chassis were impressed by the War Office. As Leyland Motors were 'working night and day to the instructions of the War Office', the MBC resorted to buying a second-hand Straker-Squire chassis (the third No.5) and two second-hand 1907 Critchley-Norris chars-a-banc (Nos.8 & 9) as replacements.

By the end of 1916, petrol, petrofein and naptha were all being used as fuel and in September 1917, bus No.9 was adapted to run on gas and fitted with a large gas-bag. The Sunday service was suspended in order to conserve fuel. When, in July 1918, a further application for petrol was refused by the Petrol Control Department, the intervention of Mr. J S Higham MP was requested and an extra 300-gallons per month were obtained.

Above: *Adorned with a pair of football boots, 1920-reconstructed ex-War Department No.9 (bearing the registration CW 1841, though officially recorded as CW 1948) waits outside the Bus Office in Church Street. Its body is thought to have been the one originally fitted to No.5 (B5771) -see page 13.*
Roy Marshall Collection/TJOC

Despite the pre-occupation with wartime restrictions, the spirit of comradeship manifested itself in a conference, convened by the Clerk to Hebden Bridge Urban District Council, between representatives of Halifax Corporation, Hebden Bridge UDC, Todmorden RDC and Todmorden Corporation, to consider 'joining up' the Todmorden bus service and the Halifax tramway service. It was recognised that no recommendations could be implemented until after the war had ended.

A slight easing of petrol restrictions enabled Sunday services to be reinstated from 5th January 1919 and following a 'general review', a completely revised timetable was introduced in May. This resulted in healthier statistics:

	April 1918	**April 1919**	**April 1920**
Miles run	7,253	8,291	11,545
Passengers carried	71,289	102,674	147,527
Receipts	£588.17s.1d	£906.10s.3d	£1,239.3s.5½d

After the war, Leyland rewarded its long standing customer by making three new RAF-type chassis available for purchase. Initially fitted with second-hand bodies, a few years later Nos.10-12 (CW 1298, CW 684 and CW 1744 - all re-issued registrations) received new Leyland bodies. It was now possible for the Corporation to resume what was to become its famous Leyland-only policy. In December 1919, Charles Moseley resigned as manager. His successor was Mr James Wild, of Edenfield, who commenced his duties as manager on 26th January 1920. Later that year, a motor-cycle was acquired for his use and a further six buses, being a combination of new, re-conditioned and second-hand Leylands, arrived in town to cope with the increased demand for travel.

Contrary to expectations, by the end of 1920 the cotton trade was experiencing one of the worst slumps in its history. Many factories were working 'short-time' and the wage rates of some employees were cut by over 25%, with an inevitable adverse effect on passenger travel. The wages of the motor bus employees were reduced by three shillings per week (a significant percentage) in September 1921 and by a further two shillings in the following May. Nevertheless, a job 'on the buses', with its absence of short-time working, was something to be prized. By November 1922, the MBC was under pressure both from the public and the Todmorden Chamber of Trade to cut fares. A fares reduction implemented in January 1923 resulted in increased passenger numbers but reduced income:

	February 1922	**February 1923**
Miles run	19,553	21,223
Passengers carried	149,726	156,273
Receipts	£1,730.15s.5½d.	£1,556.7s.9½d.

The railways, still recovering from the effects of the war, also found themselves in financial difficulties. The L&YR merged with the London & North Western Railway on 1st January 1922 and a year later became part of the giant London, Midland & Scottish Railway (LMSR).

EXPANSION OF TERRITORY AND FLEET

Expansion of its territory was seen as one answer to the financial difficulties of the bus undertaking and the issue of 'bridging the gaps' with the neighbouring systems was re-opened. Permissions were obtained from Blackshaw Parish Council to run to Whiteley Arches, from Hebden Bridge UDC to run from the arches to the Parish Church at Mytholm and from Littleborough UDC to run from Steanor Bottom to the *Summit Inn*. After receiving the necessary approvals from the West Riding and Lancashire County councils, it appears that services began running (illegally, because Todmorden's 1906 Act still only permitted buses to run within the Borough) to Mytholm and Summit on 5th August 1921.

In November 1921, Coun. John Henry Whitaker succeeded Ald. Dawson as Chairman of the MBC. The Town Clerk, Herbert Garratt, advised the MBC to apply for the necessary Provisional Order to amend the Corporation's 1906 Act in order to run services beyond the borough boundary. The matter was taken up by the council's Law & Parliamentary Committee in consultation with the Motor Bus Extension Sub-Committee and the Order received the Royal Assent on 31st July 1923, thus opening the way for negotiations with neighbouring authorities.

On 31st December 1923, the Minister of Transport granted consent to the Corporation to run buses to Hebden Bridge, Bacup and Burnley, as well as a service linking Bacup and Burnley. The Mytholm service was extended to Crown Street, Hebden Bridge on 19th January 1924. Todmorden's services to Burnley began before Burnley Corporation operated any motor bus services of its own, Burnley's first being from the Cattle Market to Abel Street on 17th March 1924. The Hebden Bridge route was an extension of the original one to Sandbed, from where it ran through the narrow gorge of the Calder, into which the road, river, canal and railway all managed to squeeze, thanks to clever engineering around the skewed Whiteley Arches.

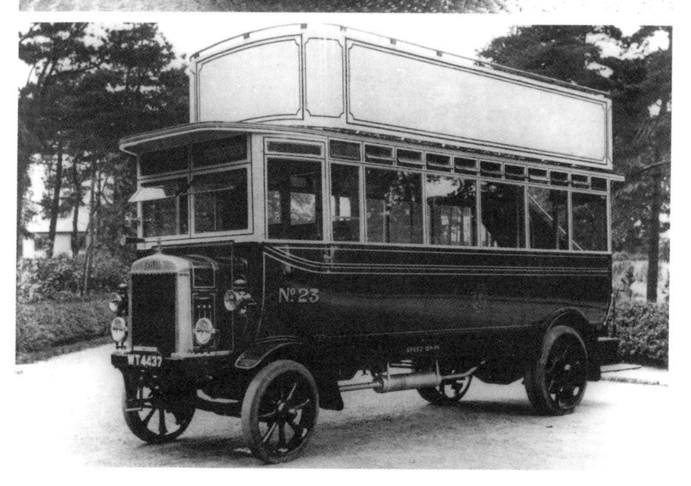

Top Right: The *1921 Leyland G2 No.14 (C 2367) has been superbly and painstakingly restored by expert vintage and veteran vehicle restorer Mike Sutcliffe, whose parents were born in Todmorden. It is seen here on 5th August 1984 at Shelf, taking part in the Trans-Pennine Rally of that year.* Don Akrigg

Middle Right: *Driving on a damp day down the middle of the A646 along York Street is the 1924 locally-bodied Leyland SG2 No.22 (WT 3608).* Roy Marshall Collection/TJOC

Bottom Right: *Leyland SG2 No 23 (WT 4437) of 1924, an early example of a 'side-type' forward-control vehicle. Note the 'SPEED 12 MPH' sign.* Roy Marshall Collection/Leyland

Above: *No.20 (WT 1843) was one of two Hickman-bodied single-deckers delivered new in January 1924 for the opening of the Todmorden-Bacup route. Here it negotiates the sharp turn from York Street into Church Street by the Corner Café*. TAS

The immediate effect of the expanded services is illustrated by the following figures:

Christmas 1923	**Passengers**	**Receipts**
Christmas Eve	8,666	£ 88 17s 10½d
Christmas Day	7,024	£ 71 9s 8d
Boxing Day	7,363	£ 72 10s 10d
	23,053	**£232 18s 4½d**

Christmas 1924	**Passengers**	**Receipts**
Christmas Eve	16,345	£ 184 13s 0d
Christmas Day	10,539	£127 2s 7½d
Boxing Day	10,829	£132 13s 11½d
	37,713	**£444 9s 7d**

The Burnley route was a six mile long extension of the original Portsmouth route, crossing the Pennine watershed via the scenic, but relatively low level, Cliviger Gorge. On the other hand, the Todmorden-Bacup and Bacup-Burnley routes severely tested both vehicles and drivers - and in both directions! The former route climbed to just over 1,300' before descending 500' to Bacup town centre. The total length of the route between Todmorden and Bacup town centres was only 5¼ miles! The latter route climbed a further 500' from Bacup along the A671 to Deerplay Moor, before descending 1,000' to Burnley, all in a distance of seven miles. Those early Leylands were certainly worked rigorously! The two routes served a number of coal mines, quarries and textile mills, as well as the three Temperleys' fireclay and sanitary pipe works between Gauxholme and Sharneyford and the Irwell Springs dyeworks near Deerplay. Initially, the buses from Todmorden entered Burnley via Towneley and Finsley Gate, while the ones from Bacup terminated at Towneley. From 1928 the latter ran into Burnley cattle market via Todmorden Road, following a miners petition.

Top Right: *Inclusion of this rather poor quality photograph, taken near Oxenhope Moor summit on the A6033, is justified on the grounds that it records the trial run to test the feasibility of the proposed Hebden Bridge-Oxenhope service. The driver is Martin Gilboy and the vehicle is the 1924 Leyland GH7 No. 26 (WT 7268). Note the two sets of bus doors and steps and the posts to show the edge of the road in snow.* TAS

Middle Right: *New to Todmorden in September 1925 were two Leyland SG11 36-seater 'half-cab' single-deckers, Nos 32 and 33. Though recorded as having the registration numbers WU 2916 and WU 2915 respectively, this photograph clearly shows No.33 as WU 2916. They were the first vehicles in the fleet to be delivered with pneumatic tyres.* Roy Marshall Collection/Leyland

Bottom Right: *Also photographed ex-works in Worden Park, Leyland, is 1928 Leyland Lion PLSC3 No.15 (WW 5574).* Roy Marshall Collection/Leyland

One could easily overlook, hidden among the minutes, a resolution passed on 5th August 1924 recommending the appointment of a youth at nine shillings per week. On the following day the MBC resolved "that the position of junior clerk in the Motor Bus Office be offered to Edward Metcalfe".

Todmorden successfully appealed to the MoT against a proposal by Ribble Motor Services to run a service from Keighley to Rochdale via Hebden Bridge and Todmorden, covering the full length of the two separated parts of the present-day A6033. Ribble tried to circumvent this by carrying passengers free of charge within the Borough of Todmorden! This antagonised not only Todmorden but also Hebden Bridge UDC, which, possibly fearing for the future of its own local services, came to Todmorden's aid by refusing to license the Ribble service through its area.

Late in 1924, with support from Hebden Bridge, Todmorden applied to run a service to Oxenhope, to connect with Keighley Corporation's existing service to that large straggling village. The route involved a long climb out of Hebden Bridge to Pecket Well on a steeply rising ledge, with an almost sheer drop to the left into the thickly wooded Hebden Vale, increasingly far below as the road climbed. The stalwart vehicles ascended from approximately 400' above sea level at Hebden Bridge to over 1,400' at the Cock Hill summit on Oxenhope Moor, then made an equally spectacular descent, with breathtaking long-range views and sharp bends into the Worth Valley. Approval for a service from Pecket Well to the village of Old Town was given on 16th April 1925. The Oxenhope service was extended to Keighley in 1927 and worked jointly with Keighley Corporation, whose bus routes became operated by Keighley-West Yorkshire Services from 1932 onwards.

Top Left: *Leviathan No.11 (WU 8326) was one of seven new Leylands purchased in 1926. Still with solid tyres, it stands on the A6033 at the Summit (Littleborough) terminus.* Roy Marshall Collection/Dennis O'Neill

Middle Left: *Also new in 1926 was Leyland SG11 No.36 (WU 8452) seen here conveying a party of shuttle makers from the Todmorden firm of John Crossley & Son, (later Crossleys Shuttles Limited), on a works outing to Chester c1928.* Frank Wilkinson (author's father)

Bottom Left: *One of nine new Leylands purchased in 1928, Titan TD1 No.7 (WW 6798) climbs out of Hebden Bridge past the junction of Bridge Lanes and Heptonstall Road, en-route to Burnley via Todmorden. The Hebble company's high-level route to Burnley via Blackshawhead followed the steep road to the left, running for many years in competition with the Todmorden low level route.* Roy Marshall Collection

Some of the new services resulted from petitions from local communities. However, a request from Heptonstall Parish Council in March 1925 for a service to Heptonstall and Colden was turned down by Todmorden; the terrain would have been particularly taxing, even for the most powerful vehicles of that period. In 1926, a service commenced via Walsden to the upland village of Lumbutts, initially on Wednesdays, Fridays and Saturdays, but later also on Sundays. Some weekend services were also extended to the neighbouring hamlet of Mankinholes.

The additional services, with their hilly routes and many steep gradients, did, of course, involve considerable additional expenditure, but they helped to provide the undertaking with a broader base over which to spread its fixed costs. In order to fulfil its many new commitments, the service embarked on a major fleet expansion as well as the recruitment of numerous additional members of staff. In each year throughout the third decade of the century, new Leylands were purchased, varying in number from one (1921 and 1922) to eleven (1924 and 1930).

The expansion of the fleet to 36 vehicles necessitated the building of a major extension to the bus garage at Millwood. This was constructed during the 1926-27 winter to plans drawn up by the Borough Surveyor to match the existing building, the height being adequate for the open-top double-deckers of the day. The Ministry of Transport sanctioned a loan of £7,000 for the purpose, but in the event only £6,500 needed to be borrowed. As a means of halting falling passenger numbers, return fares were successfully introduced on all routes in 1927. Tickets were issued on the outward journey, but were given up by the passenger to the conductor, who issued an 'Exchange Ticket' on the return journey.

Several applications by other operators to ply for hire within the Borough were turned down by the Council's Watch Committee. In one case, Claremont Omnibus Services' un-licensed Burnley to Manchester service, had to be fended off through the courts. As a result, Todmorden and Rochdale Corporations entered into negotiations concerning a jointly-operated express bus service between their two towns. This commenced on 26th January 1928, initially running as an all-day service at 40-minute intervals, the last buses being scheduled to run at 11pm from each terminus.

It is generally acknowledged that the Titan double-decker bus, with its 'piano-front' appearance and covered top, announced by Leyland in 1927, revolutionised the bus industry. Todmorden was again to the fore, taking the decision to purchase six 51-seater Titan TD1s, together with three 36-seater Lion LSC3s, all with pneumatic tyres, on 30th November 1927. The LSC3s (WW 5574-5575 and WW 5818) were delivered in March 1928 and the TD1s (WW 6759 and WW 6797-6801) during July and August 1928. Low-bridge bodies were specified for the latter because of the very low Hungry Wood arch between Cornholme and Portsmouth. Even with covered tops, the vehicles were still just able to negotiate the arch because of the unique height-saving design of its upper-deck side gangway and four-across bench seats.

The prospect of Todmorden's double-deckers having covered top decks, though still with outside rear staircases, seemed to cause concern to some neighbouring authorities (particularly Burnley) on the grounds of safety, as well as to the MoT, which was concerned about the weight of such vehicles. Following considerable correspondence, arrangements were made to reduce the weight to within the Ministry's prescribed limits. In 1928, the maximum speed limit for buses, which had to be displayed in legal lettering on the nearside of each vehicle, was increased from 12 to 20 miles per hour for vehicles having pneumatic tyres (known as pump-ups).

Top Right: *Another of the Titan TD1s was No.8 (WW 6799) delivered in 1928. They were the first Todmorden double-deckers to have covered tops. After being withdrawn from the local fleet, most of Todmorden's TD1s saw further service in Scotland.* Roy Marshall Collection/Dennis O'Neill

Middle Right: *This official Leyland view of TD1 No.4 (WW 8956), one of five new buses to enter the fleet in 1929, clearly shows the combination of covered top and open staircase.* Roy Marshall Collection/Leyland

Bottom Right: *One of eleven new vehicles acquired in 1930 was Leyland Tiger TS3 No.21 (WX 4914). Photographed ex-works, it displays the increased speed limit of 20mph for buses with pneumatic tyres.* Roy Marshall Collection/Leyland

Above: *Badly damaged, Leyland SG11 No.34 (WU 4693) completely blocks the A681 following the fatal accident in Bacup on 7th December 1928. According to contemporary reports, Driver Marshall bravely stuck to the wheel and managed to steer the bus backwards in the darkness on the slippery road at rapidly increasing speed. It ran into the old corn mill on the south side of the road before slewing round and hitting the former* Green Man Hotel. TAS

Considering the nature of the terrain and the number of vehicles operated, Todmorden's buses were involved in remarkably few serious accidents. Minor incidents in snow and ice were not unknown, but on the morning of Saturday 7th December 1928 a serious accident occurred in such conditions, when the driver of a runaway bus lost his life trying to save those of his conductor and passengers. He was Mr Will Marshall, a married man and former World War I prisoner of war, of Watty Terrace, Todmorden. The vehicle was No.34 (WU 4693), a 1926 single-decker with pneumatic tyres, operating the 6.15am service from Bacup to Cloughfoot.

About 300 yards up the first incline out of Bacup, a combination of mechanical failure and ice caused the bus to run back out of control. The Coroner praised the driver's heroism and commended the conductor, Mr. J W Greenwood of Eastwood, who advised the passengers to lie on the floor and prevented further possible loss of life by refusing to allow them to jump off the runaway bus.

In 1928, the railway companies were given greater powers to operate bus services, which were regarded as more flexible and cost-effective than many branch lines. The LMS Railway was particularly active in taking advantage of the change, taking over the Halifax to Rochdale via Blackstone Edge route, as well as buying the Hebble bus company and thus acquiring, inter alia, the Halifax to Burnley via Blackshawhead route.

Todmorden was not immune from attracting the interest of the LMSR. Discussions and negotiations proceeded for almost two years, but although there were occasional references to a manuscript minute book, the Todmorden Council and MBC minutes painstakingly avoided referring to the matter. Thus the townspeople were largely unaware of what was happening behind the scenes.

TODMORDEN JOINT OMNIBUS COMMITTEE

By 1931, Todmorden's population had fallen to just over 22,000, but it was still a vibrant, largely self-sufficient community. The MBC was just one of Todmorden Borough Council's many committees, others being Education, Electricity, Finance, Gas, Health, Highways, Hospital, Housing, Library, Parks & Recreation Grounds, Watch and Waterworks. Well over 20 sub-committees dealt with a diverse range of matters. The Corporation sold 50% of its motor bus undertaking to the London Midland & Scottish Railway (LMSR) with effect from the first day of the new decade, 1st January 1931.

Thus the Todmorden Joint Omnibus Committee (TJOC) came into being. It was one of four corporation-railway joint committees to be formed following the 1930 Road Traffic Act. All were Yorkshire based, the others being in Halifax, Huddersfield and Sheffield. Over the previous ten years, the route mileage had increased from ten, all within the Todmorden Borough boundary, to 50, extending beyond the Borough on all four sides. The reliability and comfort of the vehicles had substantially improved, as had protection for the drivers. A tender, accepted in September 1929, for tunics, trousers, caps and greatcoats for six inspectors, 50 drivers and 50 conductors, gives some indication of the number of staff then employed by the undertaking. All buses purchased from 1930 had enclosed staircases.

The Corporation's finances benefited substantially from the one-off injection of £31,250 from the sale of half the fleet. The cost of the purchase of future vehicles was only half of what it would have been under the old management, as 50% was now borne by the LMSR, but equally the railway company claimed 50% of any profits (or bore 50% of any losses). In practice, individual buses were legally owned by either the Corporation or the LMSR, but the whole was managed as a single fleet. The 50-50 balance of ownership was maintained with all new purchases. The familiar Brunswick green and cream livery was maintained, but two coats of arms now appeared on the bus sides in place of one.

Top Right: *The badge of the Corporation was joined by that of the LMSR, both being contained within an oval band which carried the words 'Todmorden Joint Omnibus Committee' in gold lettering*. Ralph Wilkinson

Middle Right: *Over 40-years after the formation of TJOC, this 1930s weather-worn bus stop sign was still performing its original function*. Ralph Wilkinson

Bottom Right: *Displaying the new TJOC emblem is 1930 Titan TD1 No.23 (WX 2074)*. Roy Marshall Collection/Dennis O'Neill

Above: *A 1932 Titan TD2, No.9 (WX 9231), cautiously negotiates Hungry Wood railway arch, between Cornholme and Portsmouth, prior to its reconstruction in 1934. The locally-made warning signs on the bridge were for the benefit of passengers on open-top double-deckers*. TAS

Rather surprisingly, no attempt was made by the Joint Committee to run buses to the LMSR's Stansfield Hall station; this could have been of benefit to both partners, as well as making it easier for the townsfolk to catch trains travelling between Yorkshire and Lancashire via the Hall Royd curve. One small but short-lived foray resulted from a request from Hebden Bridge and District Golf Club, in January 1931, to extend the Old Town service to *Mount Skip Inn*, a distance of almost 3/4 mile, on Saturdays and Sundays. The necessary application was made to the Yorkshire Area Traffic Commissioners in April; at the same time, application was made to extend the Hebden Bridge end of the service from New Road to the LMSR Station, which subsequently became the regular terminus for the Old Town and Keighley services.

The railway influence manifested itself in signs such as 'Smoking Compartment' and 'No Smoking', which began to appear in the upper and lower decks respectively, along with details of seating capacity and directives such as "Passengers must obtain ticket or tickets to the value of fare paid" or more succinctly, "Spitting Strictly Prohibited"!

One welcome event, possibly expedited by the LMSR's involvement in the bus service, was the replacement of the notorious Hungry Wood railway arch at Cornholme with a new metal girder bridge, for which a grant was allocated by the Ministry of Transport on 10th June 1933. After some delays in purchasing the necessary additional land, the contract for the work was signed in August 1934.

Top Right: *The 1932 TD2 No.11 (WX 9233) and 1930 TS3 No. 26 (WX 4915) pose for the camera near Whiteley Arches, Hebden Bridge.* TAS

Middle Right: *Leyland Tiger TS4 No.33 (YG 2038) was one of five new buses to join TJOC's fleet in December 1932.* Roy Marshall Collection/Leyland

Bottom Right: *The two 'V-fronted' TD4s, which arrived in August 1935, were never totally satisfactory and were unpopular with the drivers. Illustrated is No.38 (AWU 665).* Roy Marshall Collection/Leyland

No longer was it necessary for conductors on open-top vehicles to give verbal instructions to passengers to mind their heads! However, it was still necessary to continue to run Low-bridge buses, as the determining factor was now the height of the undertaking's own garage roof.

The TJOC made regular financial surpluses, half of which was paid into the Corporation's Motor Bus Account, and the MBC (which continued to exist, though management matters were now dealt with by the new Joint Committee) annually agreed to allocate funds from the account to the General Rate Fund. The policy of regular fleet renewal continued under the new regime. Five 51-seater Titan TD2s (WX 9231-9235) arrived in January 1932, with three more TD2s and two 36-seater Tiger TS4s (YG 2036-2040) in December. Fleet No.1 (YG 2036) had a heavy oil engine and so had only 48-seats in order to comply with the strict weight limits under the Road Traffic Act. Two TD3 and two TS6 chassis (YG 7830-7833) were bought in 1934; of each pair, one was supplied with a diesel engine and the other with a petrol engine. All future purchases had diesel engines.

Leyland experienced some difficulties with its new all-metal body, which was introduced in 1933 and for which a whole new body shop had been created in the company's South Works. Many of the vehicles sold had to be recalled and rebuilt, as the structural strength of the lower deck proved to be too weak. Leyland's body-building reputation (like many of its bodies!) was considerably dented, but the reliability of its engines and chassis was not in doubt. Consequently, the TJOC temporarily departed from its all-Leyland policy by having Northern Counties bodies fitted to the four vehicles bought in 1934. The Committee cautiously ordered two all-Leyland Low-bridge buses to be delivered in 1935. The 'V'-fronted bodies of these TD4s, Nos.37 and 38 (AWU 664-665), were built to a modified construction design intended to eradicate the problems of the earlier models and were not dissimilar in appearance to the two Northern Counties bodied double-deckers, Nos.2 and 17.

Above: *On 14th August 1938 (the first day of the service to Cross Lee), TS2 No.22 (WW 8960) dating from 1929 returns from the terminus along Cowhurst Avenue. The return route was later amended to the reverse of the outward route along Oak Avenue, presumably to avoid double-deck buses having to cross a very steep section of Ashenhurst Road at right angles.*
Roy Marshall Collection/Dennis O'Neill

By the 1930s, most other municipal transport undertakings were running buses (and in some cases trolley buses) alongside their trams. Naturally, they had begun with the latest available vehicles and, unlike Todmorden, they had not had to cope with the 'teething problems' of the infant motor bus. However, they were now having to face decisions as to which mode of transport they should adopt for the future in view of the ageing infrastructure of their tram systems; this was one problem which Todmorden did not have to face! During the 1930s, trams ceased to run in all the neighbouring vicinities: Rochdale converted its Littleborough/Summit service to bus operation on 19th October 1930; the last trams from both Rochdale and Rawtenstall ran to Bacup in 1932; Burnley's local service to Towneley was replaced by buses in 1934; and Halifax's tram service to Hebden Bridge was cut back to Tuel Lane top in 1936.

Todmorden ordered no further vehicles until the new Colin Bailey design of body, introduced by Leyland in 1936, had been well tried and tested. Ten smart new 53-seat TD5s were delivered in January 1938 and they bore the registration numbers CWR 281-290. (Their seemingly random fleet numbers continued to follow Todmorden's long standing 'gap-filling' tradition, but the numbers 39 and 40 were used for the first and only time).

Leyland had clearly set out to impress their customers with the new bodies, the most obvious improvement to the passengers being the comfortable reddish-coloured moquette seating. Six more vehicles arrived a year later: a further TD5 and five 35-seat TS8s, with light brown moquette upholstery and registered CWY 216-221.

In May 1938, application was made to the Traffic Commissioners for a licence to run the town's first local urban service. Its winding route ran via Stansfield Road, Vale Street, Wellington Road, Garden Street, Victoria Road, Park Road and Oak Avenue to Cross Lee, to serve the Corporation's new Ashenhurst housing estate.

Above: *In this typical market day scene from the late 1960s, 1950-built PD2/1 No.5 (JWY 824) leaves the Bus Starting Centre for the Summit, followed by an unidentified 1951 PD2/12 en-route to Hebden Bridge. The 'two-faced clock' (see page 41) can be seen affixed to the corner of the Market Hall.* Photobus

Right: *Stoodley Pike (inset), crowned by its peace monument forms the backdrop as 1962 Leopard No.16 (520 BWT) climbs out of Lumbutts towards Heyhead. 'Pike' is a North-country name for a hill or mountain, as in Scafell Pike. Many people think of Stoodley Pike as the stone monument, which features on the town's crest (see front cover), but the hill on which it stands has also borne that name since before even the first monument was erected on its summit in 1814.* Photobus

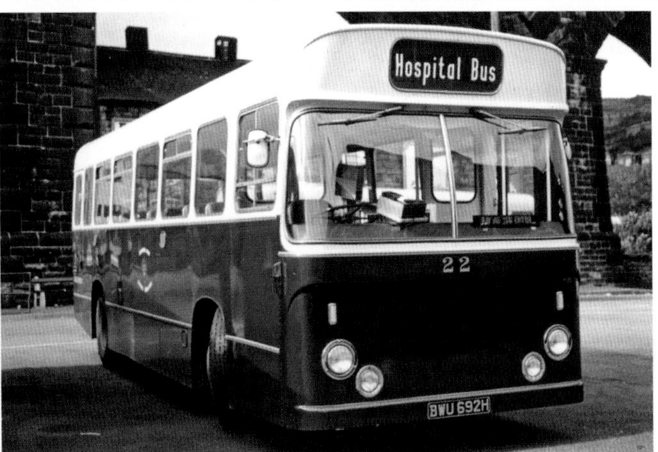

Above: *Three generations of Leylands - a historic line-up outside Millwood Bus Depot, Todmorden. From front to back: 1921 G2 Todmorden Corporation No.14 (C 2367) – see page 15; 1948 PD2/1 TJOC No.2 (GWU 12) – see page 41; 1976 FE30AGR Fleetline Yorkshire Rider Todmorden No.7006 (SUA 6R) – see page 28.* Dennis O'Neill

Left: *A 1969 Leyland PSU4A/2R, No.22 (BWU 692H), with Seddon Pennine bodywork, waits its next turn of duty in the Bus Starting Centre. The 'Hospital Bus' carried bona fide hospital visitors from Todmorden to Halifax General Hospital and the Royal Halifax Infirmary.* Photobus

Above: *A display of bus tickets: 1907 (top left and top right); 1930s 2d (centre);1940s 3d Workman (bottom left) and 10d Return (bottom right); 1960s 7d child + 1s 2d adult (bottom centre); remainder are typical 1940s and 1950s ordinary singles, some from LMSR era and others from British Railways era.* Ralph Wilkinson

Right: *A Todmorden bus in Halifax colours! Calderdale JOC adopted the livery of Halifax, which many years earlier had been copied from Glasgow. 1951 PD2/12 CJOC No.356 (KWX 18), formerly TJOC No.25, is seen approaching the Town Hall roundabout from the Halifax direction, c1972.*

Above: *In 1987, Yorkshire Rider marked the 80th anniversary of Todmorden buses by painting one of its Fleetline buses, No.7006 (SUA 6R), in the Todmorden livery of Brunswick green and cream. Looking very resplendent, it is here seen advertising a Millwood Depot Open Day. Corgi have made a model of this bus in this livery.*

Left: *EFE models of Todmorden buses. From left to right: 1947 PD2/1 No.16; 1950 PD2/1 No.19; 1930 TD1 No.23; 1964 L1 No.37; 1947 PD2/1 No.30. The position of the rear fleet number on No.16 is correct for the advertisement-carrying era-compare the picture on page 42 with that on page 22.* Alan Earnshaw

WORLD WAR II

The outbreak of World War II on 3rd September 1939 led to many restrictions, including the introduction of the blackout regulations. Indeed, as the town had been 'visited' by a Zeppelin in World War I, this was a reasonable step to take. No lighting was allowed to be visible from the air during hours of darkness and all street lighting was switched off. The glazed roofs of the platforms of Todmorden station were 'blacked out', pane by pane, making the station a very gloomy place. The amount of lighting on public transport vehicles, both inside and out, was drastically reduced and the white roofs of Todmorden's buses were painted Brunswick green. The scenario of World War I began to repeat itself: fuel rationing commenced in October 1939 and soon the effects on the bus service of staff being called up for war service were being felt.

There were fears that some of TJOC's newer vehicles might be permanently impressed for war service, but this threat did not materialise. Indeed, four new Leyland TD5s ordered in June 1939 were duly delivered in January 1940. Their seats were more deeply padded and the moquette was of a richer shade of brown than earlier TD5s. Two of the four buses dating from 1930, that these latest vehicles were intended to replace, were transferred to the Supernumerary List (WW 2074-2075) and given "X" prefixes to their fleet numbers (becoming X23 and X24). They continued to work alongside their replacements, largely on workers' services to cotton mills such as Mons (Burnley Road) and Sladen Wood (Summit). Early in the war, observant townspeople noted that at least two vehicles (X23 and 16) were absent from the local scene. Reporting in December 1940 that TJOC had lent some of their buses "to a bombed area", the *News and Advertiser* commented: "who is going to grudge a little inconvenience to help those who have suffered far more than we have done?"

Top Right: *Here we see 1938 Titan TD5 No.14 (CWR 288), one of a batch of ten which were to become the mainstay of TJOC's wartime fleet.* Roy Marshall Collection/Leyland

Middle Right: *After being withdrawn from service in 1951, 1939 Tiger TS8 No.20 (CWY 218) was re-bodied as a front entrance vehicle by Lloyds of Bagillt to give several years of further service in North Wales.* Roy Marshall Collection/Leyland

Bottom Right: *No.24 was the second of the four Titan TD5s (DWW 265-268) that entered service in 1940. They could be distinguished from the earlier TD5s by the less angular shape of the upper-deck rear dome. No. 24 (DWW 266) was superannuated in 1951, but remained in the fleet as X24 for a further nine years.* Roy Marshall Collection/Leyland

Clockwise (from top left): *Timetable Booklets and Leaflets - 1928, 1937, 1965, 1985, 1997, 2004, 2005*. Ralph Wilkinson

When the relevant clause concerning provisions for termination in the agreement with the LMS Railway of 1st January 1931 came up for review after ten years, the Corporation decided to take no action. As well as being satisfied with the *status quo*, both parties were much pre-occupied with other matters.

After more than 21 years' service, the Manager, James Wild, resigned on the grounds of ill-health as from 30th June 1941. The Joint Omnibus Committee, the Council's Motor Buses Committee and the full Borough Council all recorded appreciation of his "very valuable services". Ald. Whitaker spoke of the enormous changes in the undertaking which had taken place during Mr Wild's tenure of office. Referring to the early extensions of services, he admitted openly that at the time they were illegal, his justification being that they had led to reduced fares. He also quoted the following statistics (in round figures):

	1920	**1939**
Number of buses	9	40
Miles run	122,000	1,245,000
Receipts	£12,000	£64,000

Top Right: *An excerpt from the 1935 Timetable.*

Bottom Right: *Owing to wartime restrictions and the non-availability of film, very few photographs were taken during the early/mid 1940s. In this rare shot, 1941 Titan TD7 with Massey bodywork, No.21 (DWY 391) is seen negotiating floods outside the Olympia Cinema in Todmorden's Burnley Road.* Roy Marshall

Ald. Whitaker retrospectively justified the decision to sell half of the undertaking to the LMSR on the grounds that it had been considered "better to be partners of a successful and vigorous undertaking than to be sole owners of a languishing and declining undertaking". He paid tribute to the railway company for "having carried out the agreement to the letter". In the ten years since the formation of TJOC, the ratepayers' of the Borough had "benefited to the extent of £65,000 from the profits of the undertaking".

At a meeting of the Joint Omnibus Committee held in Crewe on 29th May, Mr. William Allen of Rochdale was appointed to the post of Manager from 1st July 1941. He could hardly have taken over at a worse time in view of the great difficulties under which the undertaking, like many others, was striving in order to keep its buses running. Further route expansion was out of the question: modest reductions in services were the best that could be hoped for under the severe restrictions imposed by the war.

In normal peacetime conditions, the Committee would have replaced the remaining four vehicles from the batch acquired in 1930. Though Leyland continued with some limited bus chassis production alongside military work, the supply of new buses for the home market was very restricted. Acute shortages of materials compounded the situation, so that when four new TD7 chassis, originally intended for the Whitehaven-based Cumberland Motor Services were diverted to Todmorden in November 1941, they arrived with unfamiliar looking Massey bodies that had timber frames made from unseasoned wood. Registered DWY 391-394, they had their rear destination blinds in a makeshift wooden 'box' in the nearside window nearest the entrance.

The replaced 1930 vehicles were given the usual 'X' prefix. Under wartime regulations, buses could not be scrapped without special permission. From 1942, these four supernumerary single-deckers (X21, X28, X29 and X32), together with five single-deckers from the current fleet, were loaned to Turner Brothers, the local coach proprietors based at Springs Garage, not far from Millwood. They were used on various War Department contracts, including some for transporting Italian prisoners of war in other parts of Yorkshire. Some of these PoWs were employed in the construction of various military and related installations between York and Selby, alongside the Derwent Valley Light Railway, whose weed-infested tracks were invisible from the air!

DO YOU KNOW?

That you may make a Circular Journey over the route—
TODMORDEN–HOLME–BURNLEY
BACUP—TODMORDEN,
At an Inclusive Fare of **2/-.**

That you can travel to Halifax with one change at Hebden Bridge at the following Return Fares:-

From TODMORDEN **1/6.**
From EASTWOOD **1/3.**

The through ticket is available on any "Hebble" or "Corporation" Bus from Hebden Bridge.

That there are good Connecting Services from Keighley to Ilkley, Otley, Skipton, &c., &c.

That children can now travel for ½d. over any Penny Stage.

Todmorden Joint Omnibus Committee

TODMORDEN CORPORATION.————L.M. & S. RLY. CO.

MILLWOOD, TODMORDEN.

Telephone No. **296.**

Top Left: *The 1934 Tiger TS6 No.15 is seen in its new role as a towing vehicle during a blizzard, possibly during the extremely severe winter of 1947. It was originally registered YG 7831, but it is here seen wearing trade plates.* TAS

Middle Left: *Here 1940 Titan TD5 No.25 (DWW 267), shows evidence of wartime bodywork patching when seen in York Street during a Driver Training exercise.* Photobus

Bottom Left: *With an 'X' prefix denoting its supernumerary status, is 1940 TD5 No.X23 (DWW 265) This vehicle remained in the fleet for a further ten years after its replacement had arrived, it waits at Lanebottom.* Photobus

Throughout the war, Todmorden managed with its existing fleet and so its passengers were spared the Spartan experiences of travelling on buses with 'utility' bodies, made to a standard wartime austerity design with hard suspension and slatted wooden seats. The fleet comprised a mixture of vehicles, several of the older ones being beyond their normal life-expectancy, though all the open-staircase buses had been disposed of by the beginning of the war. One of the 1934 Northern Counties-bodied Tiger TS6s, No.15 (YG 7831), was withdrawn from service around 1942 and its original engine used for spares. It was converted to a towing vehicle, but a report in the local paper of 1st February 1946 implies that the conversion did not take place until just after the war. Following a rescue act worthy of any fiction detective, Mike Sutcliffe is currently restoring the remains of the Tiger back to a bus.

Those many authorities that had dispensed with their electrically-propelled trams immediately before the war must, with hindsight, have regretted doing so. Whilst Todmorden did not fare so badly as some areas, the shortage of fuel forced cuts in its services nevertheless. In June 1942 the Regional Transport Commissioner required a reduction in the number of stopping places as an economy measure and the manager submitted a list to both the MBC and the JOC for approval. Priority was given to maintaining workers' services at the expense of leisure travel and late evening services. The Rochdale express service was severely curtailed, initially to four journeys per day, but by the end of 1943 it ran on Saturdays only, a pattern which was to become permanent after the war. The severe manpower shortages were addressed by the employment of four women drivers and a considerable number of conductresses.

As the war progressed, the continuing austerity began to have an increasing effect on the bus undertaking's finances, so that the size of the annual transfer from the Motor Bus Fund to the General Rate Fund diminished. In 1942 and 1943, the equivalent of a 10d. rate was transferred, but in the following two years this fell to just 6d.

Above: *The slogan 'Make do and Mend' well describes the way in which the maintenance staff of TJOC endeavoured to keep the buses in reasonable order during World War II. The author remembers a wartime journey from Todmorden to Walsden on 1932 TD2 No. 10 (WX 9232), when the driver had great difficulty in re-starting from the stop by the* Viaduct Tavern, *Gauxholme, with a full load (sitting on well-worn green leather seats) and a slipping clutch. The same vehicle is seen passing the Town Hall end of Water Street in this evocative pre-war scene.*
Copyright: Arthur Ingram

The end of the war in 1945 was marked with celebrations nationwide, but day-to-day civilian life went on much as before, with food rationing continuing - (in some cases with increased severity) - for several years. As the demobilisation programme got into full swing, many began to return home from the Forces, though sadly, as with World War I, many also did not. On 1st February 1946, a new manager took over the reins of the bus undertaking. He was William Edward Metcalfe – remember the name? Since being appointed as junior clerk in 1924, 'Teddy' Metcalfe had been promoted several times, including to Chief Clerk in 1936 and to Assistant Manager in 1940.

The post war period saw continuing shortages of raw materials and strict restrictions were placed on building repairs and developments. Industrial production was hampered by shortages of fuel, which were not helped by severe weather conditions. Todmorden's ageing fleet of buses struggled on unchanged for over two years after the end of the war as few passenger vehicles, buses or cars, were being manufactured, priority being given to export orders, lorries and other goods vehicles.

With the pending nationalisation of the railways no doubt in mind, the Corporation sought permission to apply the capital sum it had received from the sale of buses to the LMSR in 1931, in reduction of debt on the General Rate Fund Account. Following correspondence between the Town Clerk and the ministries of Transport and Health, such permission was received in April 1947 and the transfer of £31,250 from the Motor Bus Fund to the General Rate Fund was approved at a meeting of the MBC on 4th June.

Above: *Pioneer Leyland PD2/1 No.11 (FWT 183) in Grimshaw Street, Burnley, with the Burnley Building Society Head Office in the background. In his volume* The Leyland Bus, *Doug Jack, former Secretary of Leyland's Truck and Bus Division, states that "the first production PD2/1 was delivered to Todmorden Joint Omnibus Committee, complete with Leyland bodywork (L27/26R), in July 1947". An accompanying photograph shows the second production example of the chassis, also delivered to Todmorden, where, states Jack, "it entered service as No.11 in September 1947". From this, one might assume that the first production model was No.9, which entered service in August, 1947, a month ahead of the other seven members of the batch, that included No.11; however, the chassis number of No. 9 was 471592, whereas that of No.11 was the earlier one of 471277.*
R H G Simpson

Leyland again rewarded its oldest municipal customer, this time by supplying eight early production models, including the first, of a new generation of buses. The 1947 Titan PD2 series had a newly-designed engine, the 0.600, and the eight vehicles (FWT 181-188) cost a total of £29,102. Other than the deep destination blind openings, the bodywork of the PD2/1s bore a family resemblance to the pre-war classic Colin Bailey designs. The author's lasting memory of his first journey on the brand new No.9 (FWT 181), apart from the shining new paintwork, is of the quietly purring powerful engine as the vehicle effortlessly responded to each touch of the accelerator. This was in marked contrast to the straining sounds exhibited by many of the rest of the fleet. The new buses seemed to dawdle along whilst still keeping to their time schedules. (Even though the legal speed limit had been increased from 20mph to 30mph in 1931, the schedules throughout the undertaking still only averaged 12mph, with a two-person crew).

Top Right: *One of the 14 PD2/1s to enter service in February, 1948 No.21 (GWW 40), is seen in its mid-life leaving the Bus Starting Centre for Burnley with a fairly full load.* Photobus

Middle Right: *Dating from January 1950, No. 18 (HWY 36) stops in Burnley Road, Lydgate. This bus was the oldest ex-Todmorden vehicle to enter the Calderdale JOC fleet, as No.351, in 1971.* John Fozard

Bottom Right: *Looking almost like a line-up for a Leyland Motors advertisement photo-shoot, this quintet of PD2s stands in the Bus Starting Centre. From left to right: 1951 PD2/12 No.22 (KWX 15); 1950 PD2/1 No.19 (JWY 825); 1948 PD2/1 No.3 (GWW 39); 1950 PD2/1 No.8 (HWY 34); 1951 PD2/12 No.7 (KWX 12).* R H G Simpson

Having the luxury of eight additional vehicles, Todmorden was again able to loan vehicles to places less fortunate. In August 1947, 1932 TD2 No.30 (which became X30 on its replacement's arrival in the following month) went on loan to Sheffield JOC and was followed there in September by the well-travelled 1930 TD1 No.X23 and her sister No.X24, both now almost 18-years-old! With Leyland having resumed full peacetime production, no fewer than 14 new PD2/1s, in batches of eight (GWU 11-18) and six (GWW 39-44), arrived in Todmorden in February 1948. The Corporation financed its seven vehicles with the help of a loan of £20,000 from the Ministry of Transport. Eight more were added to the fleet in 1950, four in January (HWY 33-36) and a further four in November (JWY 824-827), bringing TJOC's total number of PD2/1s to 30!

Eight PD2/12s (KWX 12-19) were purchased in October 1951. The original intention to purchase four PD2/12s in the 1951-52 financial year and a further four (to replace the four 1940 TD5s) in 1952-53 was changed following an offer from Leyland to deliver all the vehicles in 1951 and to reduce the price by £140 per vehicle. The PD2/12s had eight-foot bodywork, six inches wider than the PD2/1s. The external paintwork was of a slightly lighter shade of green, with the areas around the windows on both decks coloured cream and the cream stripes below the windows removed.

These were the first buses to have the LMSR coat-of-arms replaced by the words British Railways from new, even though the LMSR had lost its identity on 1st January 1948 before all except the first eight of the PD2/1s had been delivered. The fleet now comprised 38 Titan PD2s, the oldest being only just over four-years-old, plus two supernumerary TD5s dating from 1940. For the first time in many years, there were no single-deck vehicles, all 40 buses being Low-bridge 53-seaters with open rear platform entrances (L27/26R).

BONES OF CONTENTION

Within months of the end of World War II, letters pressing for a through bus service between Todmorden and Halifax appeared in the local press. A particular bone of contention was the lack of co-ordination between timings of the TJOC and Halifax JOC services at Hebden Bridge. Further correspondents complained about the similar situation at Summit, where the timings of the Todmorden and Rochdale buses were not synchronised. Those returning after several years of enforced absence with HM Forces were bewildered to discover that their fellow townsfolk back home seemed to have nothing better to do than complain about waiting for a few minutes for a bus! Of genuine concern were the difficulties in reaching the two major Halifax hospitals, a time-consuming exercise for which three separate buses each way were necessary. It was not until August 1947 that a regular Sundays only direct service from Todmorden, picking up only between Todmorden and Eastwood, was established for hospital visitors.

Another hot topic, which rumbled on from early 1946, was the absence of bus shelters. Todmorden began to acquire the dubious reputation of being one of the first places to get buses, but one of the last to get bus shelters!

Passengers' hopes were raised when, on 2nd February 1949, the MBC deferred making an allocation from the Motor Bus Fund to the General Rate Fund until a decision was made on the question of the provision of bus shelters, but at the Council meeting on 26th October 1949, a motion by Coun. Herbert Hardy "that this Council consider erecting bus shelters in the Borough", was lost.

Top Left: *A bone of contention in the days before the bus station was the parking in town centre streets of buses between duties. Between the wars, Dale Street was a favourite location for this practice until the Todmorden Industrial & Co-operative Society, whose main stores and Head Office dominated the street, raised objections. In this shot, taken on 14th April 1952, TD5 No.X23 is seen 'parked up' in Station Road. It is possible that the bus was on stand-by for a train substitution service.* Roy Marshall

Middle Left: *At the almost identical spot are a pair of PD2/1s awaiting their next duties. The metal girder bridge abutting the railway viaduct carried the rail spur into the bay platform, which served trains terminating/commencing their journeys from/to Preston, Blackburn and Burnley until that service was withdrawn in November 1965.* Photobus

Bottom Left: *In August 1954, PD2/12 No.20 (KWX 14) waits for time at the bus shelter by the Burnley Valley starting point outside the Abraham Ormerod Medical Centre.* John Fozard

Undaunted, Coun. Raymond Law, who had supported the motion, provided a shelter at his own expense by installing windows and seating in an existing building on his own land at Lanebottom. Alderman William Egerton believed that it was the responsibility of the bus operator (TJOC) to provide shelters, but he was taken to task by a resident who pointed out that Bacup Council, which had no buses of its own, had built shelters at the most needed points.

On 29th March 1950, the Council resolved "to take steps to erect a temporary bus shelter at the Medical Centre, Burnley Road, and approach the TJOC for a contribution", but no shelter materialised. On 6th June 1951, the MBC approved "in principle" the erection of a shelter at the Medical Centre and set up a Bus Shelter Sub-committee "to consider the type of shelter and to act". The Abraham Ormerod Medical Centre was one of the town's prized possessions.

Above: *Todmorden's controversial bus shelter is again seen in this view of 1947 PD2/1 No.9 (FWT 181) and 1951 PD2/12 No.7 (KWX 12) operating to Burnley.* Photobus

Built on the site of the former Ridgefoot Mill, it had been given to the citizens by the trustees of the late cotton manufacturer whose name it bore. It had been opened by HRH The Princess Royal in 1938; thus, in 1951 it was still a relatively new building, designed and built by proud Todmordians. The Council could hardly have chosen a more sensitive location and it might be assumed that the sub-committee's brief was to approve a building worthy of its environment. What emerged was a pre-fabricated concrete and armoured glass structure, open to the elements at the town end. Nevertheless, Todmorden had a bus shelter: all that was lacking was an official opening by a member of the Royal Family.

Above: *Supervised by the figures on the pediment of the Town Hall, buses for Summit, Walsden and Bacup jostle for space in narrow Church Street. Despite the obvious dangers, Ald. Whitaker fought strongly to retain the bus starting points, claiming that Church Street was the safest place in Todmorden and that one could cross it on one's hands and knees without taking any harm! As the local paper stated more prosaically in its issue of 25th July 1947, the points at issue were traffic congestion and road safety balanced against the convenience of a large number of bus passengers. The problem was still unresolved when the author took this 'snap' of Nos.27, 9 and 4 with a pre-war Brownie box camera in 1952!* Ralph Wilkinson

A further bone of contention was the starting point for the town's bus routes, which for many years was the Town Hall. As the times of the three main services coincided, connections worked smoothly. Services from Burnley (or, in some cases, Portsmouth) ran alternately to Summit and Hebden Bridge, those from Summit alternately to Hebden Bridge and Burnley, and those from Hebden Bridge alternately to Burnley and Summit. Thus, with a 15-minute interval service, there were through buses between each valley every half-hour, and on the intervening quarters it was simply necessary to cross the road at the Town Hall to join the appropriate connecting service.

As traffic increased, the waiting buses began to cause congestion. In North Street (Burnley Road), the Cross Lee terminus remained by the junction with Station Road, but the Burnley and Portsmouth starting point was moved to the *Black Swan Hotel*. Connections became slightly less convenient, but still practicable. In the Spring of 1947, the Traffic Commissioners ordered the bus stops in the town centre to be re-located a few yards further away from the Town Hall.

Todmorden Accident Prevention Council registered to the Commissioners its concern with the situation in Church Street (Rochdale Road), which was the starting point for the Summit, Walsden, Bacup, Lumbutts and Rochdale services, as well as the regular services operated by Ribble Motor Services. For much of the time, it was not possible for two streams of traffic to pass in the narrow street, which was used by many heavy goods vehicles in the days before the opening of the M62 motorway.

In 1946, Thomas Sharp, a town planning consultant, recommended that a main road be constructed linking the Halifax and Burnley roads, by-passing the Town Hall, and that a bus station be built to the west of it, near the viaduct. In July 1947, the Council's Watch Committee became aware of the poor condition of some buildings, located under the viaduct, which were owned by the Council. It was suggested that, if these were cleared, a temporary bus station could be made pending implementation of the Sharp Plan, but the main Council considered the suggestion to be impracticable.

Two years later, the MoT proposed that the starting point for the Burnley valley buses be moved to the Medical Centre and that for the Cross Lee service to a point immediately beyond the railway viaduct. There was widespread agreement that this would make town centre connections difficult. However, whilst Coun. Hardy believed that the proposal strengthened the case for a bus station, Ald. Whitaker reminded councillors that it was still the Council's view that a bus station was impracticable. Coun. Leo Cockcroft stated that he did not wish to discuss the question of a bus station except to state that it would require a lot of money, making it essential to acquire a loan from the Ministry. In February 1946, the MBC had contributed £4,059 to the relief of rates for the year 1946-47, bringing the total since the inception of TJOC in 1931 to around £84,000, but financial problems had now begun to impinge upon the bus service. The last transfer took place in 1950.

Top Right: *For many years, Todmorden's buses entered Burnley's Cattle Market bus station via Parker Lane and departed via Grimshaw Street. Shortly after commencing their journeys to Hebden Bridge and Bacup respectively, 1951 PD2/12 No.7 (KWX 12) and 1950 PD2/1 No.26 (JWY 826) rejoin their inward route in St. James's Street, since pedestrianised, in 1954.* Roy Marshall

Middle Right: *Seen from near the circular end of the Town Hall, PD2/1 No.17 (GWU 14) proceeds along North Street to the new starting point for the Cross Lee service.* R H G Simpson

Bottom Right: *Here PD2/12 No.25 (KWX 18) waits for time at the Hebden Bridge starting point outside Martin's Bank at the corner of York Street and Bridge Street.* Photobus

Top Left: *All 30 of the post-war PD2/1s remained in the TJOC fleet until at least the 1960s. After being superannuated, 1947 No.12 (FWT 184) served for another ten years with Barton Transport from 1962! It is seen here in Nottingham in its new livery as Barton Fleet No.943.*

Middle Left: *Dating from February 1948, No.28 (GWW 41), which also joined the Barton fleet (as No.942) from 1962 to 1972, stands in York Street outside the* Wellington Inn. *One of its sisters still survives. On being withdrawn from service in 1970, 1948 No.2 (GWU 12) - see photograph on next page - was bought by Todmorden Antiquarian Society for preservation. Since then No.2 has been carefully restored by David Powell, of Todmorden, in whose care it now resides.* John Fozard

Bottom Left: *No.5 (JWY 824), new in November 1950 despite wearing the LMSR badge, became CJOC No.352 in 1971. It was later sold to Mulley's Motorways Ltd, Ixworth, where it remained in service until 1977, thus probably establishing the record for longevity of any Todmorden bus in regular service. It is seen here outside the main post office in Burnley Road, Bacup.* Photobus

In an attempt to save money, ordinary and workman return fares were abolished in January 1953. The need for TJOC to make further economies resulted, after lengthy staff negotiations, in a change of frequency in the three core routes from 15 minutes to 20 minutes. Introduced in December 1956, this facilitated better connections at Hebden Bridge and Summit, but the tightening of journey times (a saving of five minutes in every 45) led to less time being available for passengers to catch Todmorden town centre connections, with inevitable further discontent among the public.

Extensive road works in the town centre early in 1957 caused the Police to request the Town Clerk and the Chairman of the Markets and Lighting Committee to grant the immediate use of the market ground as a temporary departure point for all buses, except those to the Burnley valley and Cross Lee. This fortuitous intervention caused all concerned to experience at first-hand the advantages of a central starting point.

The Borough Surveyor was asked to provide a suitable lamp to illuminate the rear portion of the ground at an estimated cost of £15 and to provide signs indicating the various termini. Thus, for a few pounds and without the need for a Ministry loan, the town had a makeshift bus station! Two years later, the bus termini were re-arranged to accommodate the Burnley valley services within the Bus Starting Centre, whereupon the Cross Lee starting point was moved forward to the now vacant bus shelter at the Medical Centre. Accommodation for bus crews and inspectors was provided at a cost of around £500.

Above: *Until the frequency of TJOC's core services was reduced from four to three buses per hour in 1956, only one in four of TJOC's services connected conveniently with Rochdale Corporation's services at the* Summit Inn. *Rochdale's vehicles wore a smart -blue and white streamlined livery. The Todmorden bus in this 1954 picture has since been preserved - see previous page and also page 26.* Roy Marshall

In December 1959, the Borough Surveyor was asked to prepare a scheme for the erection on the market ground of four concrete and glass shelters, one for each stand, making use of existing walls as far as practicable. The new Bus Starting Centre (the term 'Bus Station' was meticulously avoided in all Council records) was deemed by almost everyone to be a great success. However, some members of the MBC, while publicly accepting the ratepayers appreciation, were still hankering after roadside starting points some years later! In 1961, quotes were sought for a "two-faced" clock to be placed on the north-west corner of the Market Hall. Whether the committee members saw the irony of this description of a double-dial clock is unrecorded! In 1963, the Inspectors' Hut was enlarged to accommodate an Enquiry Office and the old office in Church Street was closed. Thus, at a total cost of around £2,000, the Bus Starting Centre (bus station in all but name) was complete.

The public became visually aware of TJOC's deteriorating financial situation when advertisements began to appear on the outside of the buses. The first, in 1959, were anti-litter posters as part of the 'Keep Britain Tidy' campaign, but in 1960 commercial advertisements were displayed for the first time since 1912.

It is worth noting in passing that, in November 1962, Pearl & Dean Ltd wrote to the Corporation offering to provide bus shelters free of charge in return for advertising rights. Suddenly, all the arguments over bus shelters evaporated and discussions between Council representatives and the company's Northern Area Manager were reported upon enthusiastically. Negotiations subsequently broke down, partly because of lack of agreement over the suitability of the suggested sites, after which the Council embarked on a long-term programme of providing shelters itself. Finally, following requests for seats in the bus shelters at the Bus Starting Centre, the Council eventually agreed to provide a single seat! Todmorden Rotary Club provided seats for the other three shelters in 1967.

Above: *Here PD2/1 No.4 (GWU 13) looks like a mobile advertising hoarding as it waits at the Hebden Bridge stand in the Bus Starting Centre, adjacent to the Market Hall, in the early 1960s.* John J. Holmes

THE FINAL YEARS

The post-war increase in motor car ownership resulted in less people using bus services throughout the country, but the situation in places like Todmorden was exacerbated by further textile mill closures and a continuing decline in the population.

	1950-51	1960-61	% Reduction
Miles run	1,300,000	1,124,000	13.54
Passengers carried	10,590,00	6,846,000	35.36

The above reduction in mileage was largely a result of the change from 15-minute to 20-minute frequencies on the main routes. Yet, despite regular fare rises, further drastic action was needed. Many other undertakings were able partially to address the problem by the introduction of one-person operated buses, but Todmorden, with its all double-decker rear-entrance fleet, did not have a single vehicle suitable for such use.

In April 1961, the TJOC's first new bus for ten years and first post-war single-decker, was delivered. Registered 634 WY, it was a 44-seater Leyland Leopard L1 costing £4,660. It was initially employed on the Old Town service, but met with an accident during its first few weeks of operation, so the one-person experiment got off to a bad start. Four similar new L1s were purchased, two (520-521 BWT) in September 1962 and two (572-573 EYG) in January 1964. All five had East Lancashire (of Blackburn) bodywork, Leyland having ceased building bodies in December 1954.

Passenger numbers were much reduced on the Todmorden-Bacup and Bacup-Burnley routes, where most of the coal mines and other industrial enterprises had closed.

Top Right: The year of *1961 saw the arrival of TJOC's first single-decker since the 1939 batch of Leyland Tiger TS8s. After setting down a couple of passengers, Leyland Leopard L1 No.12 (634 WY) is about to negotiate the very sharp right-hand turn from the A6033 at Pecket Well on the Hebden Bridge station to Old Town route*. Photobus

Middle Right: *Advertising Dulux paints (see page 41), PD2/12 No.22 (KWX 15) stops to pick up a passenger at Dyneley Road, between Walk Mill and Towneley. The bridge carries the Todmorden-Burnley railway line. In later years, buses on service 595 continued to follow this route, but those on services 589 and 592 diverted from the A646 at Walk Mill to enter Burnley via Mereclough and Pike Hill, as do all services today.*
Robert F. Mack

Bottom Right: *An almost empty 1964 Leopard L1, No.29 (572 EYG), leaves Burnley Cattle Market bus station in the final months of the TJOC-operated Burnley-Bacup service. Note the Hebble vehicle on a sparsely-supported Burnley-Halifax via Blackshawhead Service 15. Passengers for Leeds changed to a double-decker vehicle at Halifax, though Route 15 was officially a 'through' service from Burnley to Leeds.*
Robert F. Mack

Some mileage was saved by service reductions in April 1964, but a request to Bacup Council for a subsidy of around £2,000 per year to keep the remaining services running was turned down. The services were withdrawn on 6th March 1966, after which Ribble and Rossendale provided a joint service between Sharneyford and Bacup. Meanwhile Ribble took over the Bacup-Burnley route. Todmorden provided a local service as far as Cloughfoot, but some services were later extended to Sharneyford. The cuts had the intended effect of reducing TJOC's total miles travelled by a greater percentage than the total number of passengers carried.

Nevertheless, the financial position of TJOC was causing increasing concern. Following a report by the Borough Treasurer, on 17th August 1966 the MBC authorised the transfer from the Motor Bus Account to the credit of TJOC of a half-share of any money required by the Joint Committee for working capital. Payback time had arrived!

Discussions with Halifax JOC (commenced in 1966) resulted in a small but significant development. For many years, children from Todmorden travelling to Calder High School had had to change buses in Hebden Bridge twice daily and parents renewed demands for a through service. Thus, despite objections from Hebble, a jointly operated (TJOC/HJOC) service at school times was introduced between Todmorden and Halifax from 15th May 1967.

Above: *A variety of buses queue to leave the Bus Starting Centre, led by 1967 Leopard L1 No.9 (NWW 89E) on a heavily-loaded one-man-operated service to Burnley. The familiar double-crested TJOC logo has been replaced by the single coat-of-arms of Todmorden Corporation following the transfer of British Railways' interest to APT. This Willowbrook-bodied vehicle has since been preserved privately by John Flowers. One of its dual-purpose bodied sisters, cream-painted No.10 (NWW 91E), can just be seen operating the service to Summit.* Online Transport Archive

The 19th May 1967 issue of the *Todmorden Courier* (a short-lived weekly newspaper) displayed a front page photograph of Halifax's No.288, showing Route 44 and the destination 'Mytholmroyd', operating the new service. So after 60-years of buses in Todmorden and several aborted discussions, it was possible to travel by bus from Todmorden to Halifax without changing, though still only at certain times of the day!

By the end of 1966, six of the eight 1947 PD2/1s and seven of the 14 purchased in 1948 had been withdrawn. Four new Leyland Leopard L1s with Willowbrook bodies (NWW 88E-91E) were delivered in February 1967. The first two (Nos.4 and 9) had conventional bus bodies, but, with the prospect of private hire work in mind, the last two (Nos.1 and 10) had all-cream dual-purpose bus/coach bodywork.

As a result of the 1968 Transport Act, the British Rail representatives of the Joint Omnibus Committee were replaced by nominees of Amalgamated Passenger Transport Limited (APT), a subsidiary of the National Bus Company (NBC). Two second-hand 44-seater Leyland Tiger Cub PSUC1s, dating from 1956 and 1958, were acquired in July 1969 from East Midland Motor Services, itself an NBC company. Later that year, six new Leyland Leopard PSU4As with Seddon Pennine bodywork (BWU 688H-693H) were delivered. The first two (No.6 and 8) were dual-purpose vehicles with enhanced seating.

Further vehicles were desperately needed, but not all the routes were considered suitable for one-person operation, so in March 1970 TJOC authorised the Manager to acquire three second-hand single-deck vehicles and ten second-hand double-deck vehicles. Thus, three second-hand Leyland Leopards with Eastern Coach Works bodies (1880-1882 WA), dating from April 1961 and originally new to Sheffield JOC, came to Todmorden via the auspices of APT in August 1970.

Top Right: *The second of the pair of second-hand Tiger Cubs with MCCW bodywork, acquired from East Midland Motor Services Limited, of Chesterfield leaves the Summit terminus. Behind it can be seen Summit brickworks, its associated clay quarry and the* Summit Inn. *The Tiger Cubs were found to be under-powered for TJOC's more rugged routes and so were restricted to lower level terrain.* Photobus

Middle Right: *Dual-purpose vehicle No.6 (BWU 688H), one of the1969 Leopards from the Leyland zoo, sets off from the Bus Starting Centre for Hebden Bridge on 13th April 1971 along the North Street section of Burnley Road.* Roy Marshall Collection

Bottom Right: *One of the final trio of ex-Sheffield buses to enter the fleet (in 1970), No.2 (1880 WA) awaits its departure time for Lumbutts on 9th April 1971. Their ECW coach-style bodies were not adapted for one-man-operation, so they were employed mainly in place of double-deckers.* Roy Marshall

These were to be the last of the almost 200 vehicles to enter the Todmorden fleet. Acquisition of the ten second-hand double-deckers was put on hold in view of uncertainties about the future of TJOC. Whereas at the beginning of the 1960s the fleet had been all double-deck, by the end of the decade the majority of vehicles were single-deck, but the fleet was still all-Leyland.

The F&GPC agreed to the money in the Motor Bus Account, currently used for general Corporation purposes, being made available for bus purposes. Further contributions towards TJOC's working expenses were authorised in May and December 1967 by the long standing Motor Bus Committee, which ceased to exist with effect from the beginning of the 1968-69 local government year. All bus matters were now dealt with by the F&GPC, which immediately took a greater interest in the financial aspects of the bus undertaking and the Council's future financial liabilities towards it.

The annual accounts of TJOC for 1967-68 were considered in detail and at the F&GPC's 20th November meeting the Borough Treasurer was asked to arrange for TJOC's eight-weekly financial statements to be circulated to members, thus reviving a practice that had not taken place since 1930! Consideration of the future of the Motor Bus undertaking was twice deferred (in April and October 1969). The loan of £25,000 from the Motor Bus Fund to the Council's General Fund was repaid in order to pay for the Corporation's share of the six new buses delivered in November and December 1969. Concern was expressed that no financial provision was made for the purchase of new vehicles and in March 1970 the F&GPC resolved that "in future Motor Buses owned by the Corporation be depreciated on the basis of a 12-year life".

Above: *Transition time, 1971. The town centre railway viaduct overlooks this trio of Leyland single-deckers with their new Calderdale Joint Omnibus Committee numbers. The 1956 Leopard PSUC1/1 No.339 (URR 355), ex-Todmorden No.11 and previously East Midland No.R355, finds itself between 1969 Leopard PSU4A/2Rs Nos.331 (BWU 691H), ex-Todmorden No.19, and 333 (BWU 693H), ex-Todmorden No.23. No.333 has already been re-painted into the green, orange and cream livery of CJOC, while the others still wear their Todmorden colours.* Ralph Wilkinson

Discussions concerning major restructuring of the bus industry took place during the late-1960s. In a chapter of his recently published second part of *Steel Wheels and Rubber Tyres* Volume 2 (Oakwood Press, 2004) headed 'Wide Horizons-Todmorden Merger', Mr Geoffrey Hilditch, who as Halifax General Manager was much involved in the process, says: "This part of the story had a beginning at one of those Transport Conferences, this one taking place in Scarborough in 1968 when the Chairman of the Todmorden Joint Omnibus Committee, who then represented the Municipal side of that concern, came up to my Chairman and I and said with a smile, Want to buy a bus undertaking? The manner was jocular, but there was obviously some purpose behind the approach. We countered with a few questions of our own and it came to pass thereafter that more serious discussions began in other places".

The eventual outcome was a merger between the Halifax and Todmorden undertakings, formally agreed at a meeting in Halifax Town Hall on 17th March 1971. On Edward Metcalfe's retirement a few weeks later, Geoffrey Hilditch became Acting General Manager of Todmorden. In anticipation of the merger, proposed for 6th September 1971, the 27 Todmorden vehicles expected to be transferred to the merged undertaking were re-numbered during April and May in the series 331-357 by the application of oval stickers carrying black numbers on a white background.

At a meeting of the Calderdale Joint Omnibus Steering Committee on 29th July 1971, Mr Hilditch was appointed as the proposed new Calderdale JOC's General Manager and Aldermen Leo Cockcroft and Alfred King were nominated as members designate of CJOC to represent Todmorden Corporation.

Top Right: *Still in its TJOC dual-purpose livery, but showing its new CJOC number 327, former Todmorden Leopard No.10 (NWW 91E) is framed by some interesting advertisements as it loads passengers for the Burnley Valley alongside the viaduct.* Travel Lens Photographic

Middle Right: *Ex-Halifax (RCP 277K) but later CJOC No.297, was one of the batch of 11 new Daimler Fleetline CRG6LX double-deckers allocated to Todmorden's Millwood depot in 1972. It looms large when pictured here as it pauses in Todmorden en-route from Burnley to Rochdale.*

Bottom Right: *CJOC No.355 (KWX 17, formerly Todmorden's PD2/12 No.24), now 20-years-old but still in service, looks diminutive as it stands in its new livery alongside ex-Halifax 1959 Leyland PD3/4 No.202 (KCP 11).* John Fozard

It was also agreed that the livery of CJOC's vehicles should be the orange, cream and green colours of the Halifax fleet, less the Halifax coat of arms, so some of the ex-Todmorden vehicles were repainted in this livery. One condition of the merger was that the average age of the fleets should be not more than seven years, so a number of exchanges of vehicles took place within the fleets to reduce the average age of the Todmorden fleet to the required level!

Services were fully integrated from 27th September 1971, three weeks after the date of the merger. Route numbers were introduced and all-day through services began to operate along the Calder Valley. Halifax had relatively few low-bridge vehicles, so two second-hand low-bridge AEC double-deckers, bought from Maidstone & District, arrived in Todmorden as a temporary measure. A Halifax order for new vehicles was suspended and the specification altered to provide 12 new Daimler CRG6LX rear-engined 75-seater double-deck vehicles for CJOC. Eleven of these were allocated to Millwood and went into service between May and July 1972, thus transforming the appearance and comfort of the Todmorden-based section of the fleet in less than a year after the merger had taken place!

All municipally-operated services in the new Metropolitan County of West Yorkshire, which came into being on 1st April 1974, were transferred to the West Yorkshire Passenger Transport Executive (WYPTE, trading as 'Metro') on that date. A new livery of Cream and Verona Green was eventually adopted throughout the county. The 16 surviving ex-TJOC vehicles were renumbered 3323-3338 in the Metro fleet. In 1980, the fleet name was changed to 'Metrobus'. Following the deregulation of bus services in 1986, the WYPTE transferred its own bus operations to a new company, Yorkshire Rider Limited, which adopted another new green and cream livery, not too dissimilar from Todmorden's former colours.

Top Left: *Operating on the lengthy but short-lived CJOC 'Flagship' Route 8 (Burnley-Todmorden-Halifax-Leeds), CJOC No.356 (KWX 18, formerly TJOC No.25) is caught on camera in Halifax.* John Fozard

Middle Left: *This 1987 Freight Rover Sherpa Yorkshire Rider No.1796 (D796 KWR), in 'Micro Rider' livery, stands in a deserted Todmorden Bus Station, as the former 'Bus Starting Centre' became known officially.* 6809 Group

Bottom Left: *This 1976 Leyland Leopard PSUD/4R Yorkshire Rider Todmorden No.8534 (RWU 534R) enters Millwood Bus Depot, Todmorden, after working Route 500 to Keighley. It is seen painted in the former TJOC livery, in which it was to remain in service in the town until 1999!* Copyright: Tony Greaves

Once more the local buses based at Millwood Depot carried the town's name as part of their fleet name 'Yorkshire Rider Todmorden'. Following a management buy-out in 1988, Yorkshire Rider became a private sector company. Six years later, it was purchased by the Badgerline Group and in June 1995 Badgerline and Grampian merged to form 'FirstBus'. A new livery, predominantly white, with blue and yellow bands, was adopted for FirstBus Calderline services in 1998, and in the following year the first vehicles in the new corporate livery of FirstBus plc began to appear. This white, blue and rubine red colour scheme has been applied progressively to all First vehicles as repainting has become due.

Various route changes have taken place in recent decades. As early as the summer of 1971, Geoffrey Hilditch entered into talks with Rossendale and Ribble about the possibility of a joint Todmorden-Bacup service. Thus TJOC's former pioneering service between the two towns was re-instated as CJOC's Route 93. (It is currently operated by Rossendale as Route 49, with WYPTE and Lancashire County Council support, but is again under threat). An experimental service to the Longfield estate, began on 24th June 1974 less than three months after the establishment of Metro. This was followed by a number of other town services.

The introduction of mini-buses, initially Freight Rover Sherpas in 'Microrider' livery, made it possible to expand the routes to places that the larger vehicles could not reach. The Mankinholes service became a circular route operating via Springside, Harvelin Park, Lumbutts and Walsden and vice versa. With financial support from Metro and the Government's Rural Bus Scheme, a network of local services now operate under the MetroConnect banner serving places such as Carr House Estate, Highcroft, Kilnhurst, Dineley Avenue (a variation on the Cross Lee route), Todmorden Station and Morrisons' supermarket.

A similar network of local services operates in Hebden Bridge. These run to new destinations such as Eaves, Fairfield, Foster Lane and Dodd Naze, as well as traditional places such as Blackshawhead, Cragg Vale and Hardcastle Crags.

Metro, no doubt with helpful intentions, has provided new bus stop signs. These aim to identify the names of the stops, but several bear little relation to the traditional names or have simply been erected in the wrong places, thus adding a new twist to Metro's slogan, 'Here to get you there'!

To be fair to Metro and First, the main services through the valley have improved, despite the continuing increase in car ownership. Many services have been re-numbered and today, as part of a colour-coded Overground scheme for key routes in Calderdale, First Green Line services operate a ten-minute interval service from Halifax to the Upper Calder Valley (Services 590-594). Of the six buses per hour to Hebden Bridge, one goes to Heptonstall and one to Old Town, while the remaining four proceed to Todmorden. Of these four, one goes forward to Rochdale and one to Burnley. Rochdale and Burnley are also linked via Todmorden by an additional hourly First service and a further half-hourly service is operated between Burnley and Todmorden by Burnley-based Northern Blue.

The Bus Starting Centre, now officially Todmorden Bus Station, was enlarged towards Stansfield Road in 1996 and is straddled by the viaduct. Photographs, plans of its layout, and other details can be seen worldwide via the internet. It is served by all buses in the town, including a fleet of 18 state-of-the-art, easy-access, double- and single-deck Volvo Wright Eclipse buses, which First introduced for the Green Line services in August 2005 at a cost of £2.5 million. What would those patient townsfolk who waited at the Town Hall to see Todmorden's first Critchley-Norris on 1st January 1907, or even those who witnessed the last TJOC-operated buses in 1971, have made of all that?

Top Right: *1988 Leyland Olympian ONCL10/1RZ Yorkshire Rider Todmorden No.5156 (F156 XYG). For several years this vehicle was painted in the former TJOC livery, but is here seen in its conventional Yorkshire Rider Todmorden colours at Burnley Bus Station on Service 589 to Rochdale. It was one of a batch of 12 buses that bore the former Borough of Todmorden coat-of-arms on their front grilles.* Author's Collection

Bottom Right: *Here we see the face of the 21st century as a 2005 Volvo Wright Eclipse No.32537 (YJ05 VUX) passes beneath the town centre viaduct. It is entering the bus station* en-route *from Burnley to Halifax on Green Line Service 592 on 29th April 2006. Todmorden's services today are operated by the giant road and rail travel group, First.* Ralph Wilkinson

Above: En-route *for Mankinholes, one-man-operated 1962 Leopard No.16 (520 BWT) has just rounded the long right-hand bend between California and Swineshead on its climb out of the Rochdale Valley up Lumbutts Road. The A6033 Rochdale Road, along which it would have travelled between Waterside and Shade some ten minutes earlier, is hidden in the deep valley at the lower right of the picture, while the A681 Bacup Road is hidden deep in the fold of the hills at the extreme upper left. Pexwood Road, leading to Stones and Dobroyd, can be seen at the upper right.* Photobus

DE REBUS OMNIBUS

However accurately one might try to describe the vehicles, the routes and the events, which together provide a historical record of Todmorden's pioneering bus service, there were additional trivia and intangible elements that contributed to the whole. Some odd questions remain unanswered: why, for example, did generations of Todmorden Grammar School pupils refer to the Cross Lee bus as the 'Clipper'? Incidentally, during the author's time there as a pupil, the half-price (child) fare from the school at Ferney Lee to the Town Hall was just 1/2d (0.2p).

On hilly routes in snowy weather, it was often the practice for waiting passengers to space themselves out along the road. Drivers would run slowly past the line and the passengers would deftly jump on to the open platform of the moving bus when it reached them. Miners in the Bacup area were particularly adept at this and were also known for being considerate of other passenger's needs: when material-upholstered seats were introduced, miners returning home from work often stood, even though seats were available, in order not to dirty the upholstery.

A regular traveller on the Lumbutts route was known by his fellow passengers for his practice of alighting from the bus at Copperashouse and walking leisurely up Parsons Brow, which links Rochdale Road and Hollins Road, to rejoin the same vehicle on its same journey several minutes later at the bottom of Lumbutts Road. He claimed to do it for the exercise, but it was thought more likely that his motive was to save a halfpenny on the fare! The accompanying photograph gives some indication of the terrain in question.

Top Right: *The 1967 Leopard CJOC No.326 (NWW 90E, formerly Todmorden No.1) stands at the Cross Lee terminus in its original TJOC dual-purpose livery. A Halifax-style bus stop sign has replaced that of TJOC, which was previously fixed to the lamp-post. The Burnley Valley can be seen in the left distance.* Photobus

Middle Right: *Temperley's Saunder Clough fireclay works dominates the scene as an earlier Todmorden No.1 (GWU 11, of 1948) climbs the steep A681 Bacup Road towards the county and borough boundary at Sharneyford. For a number of years, Ribble's daily Todmorden-Blackburn-Blackpool Service X97 followed this route between May and September.* John Fozard

Bottom Right: *In this scene from the 1960s, TJOC 1950 PD2/1 No.18 (HWY 36) is about to enter the Bus Starting Centre as Leeds City Transport 1955 Leyland Tiger Cub No.29 (TUA 29) passes along Burnley Road on a charter hire.* Robert F. Mack

Lip-reading, which was the normal means of communication in a noisy weaving-shed, could be a useful asset outside work. Visitors witnessing a woman standing at a bus stop 'talking' in this manner to a man on the top deck of a bus might have wondered what highly confidential or clandestine piece of information was being communicated, whereas most locals following the silent exchange would know that she was merely asking her husband to "bring 'alf a pound o'tripe from Redmans".

The friendliness of the staff and the banter between the conductors and regular passengers, which visitors might have considered over-familiar, remain in the memory of many locals in general and this author in particular. In the days before calculators or automatic ticket machines, virtually everyone was able to perform routinely, what today would be regarded as quite complex tasks of mental arithmetic. Courtesy was also evident as well. On being asked for 'two adults and three children to X', the conductor would answer correctly and instantaneously (in non-decimal currency,) and his/her reply would not be questioned. On full buses, it was normal practice for children to give up their seats to adults, without needing to be asked.

Mention has been made of petitions for bus services from rural areas. It is reputed that on one such petition from a remote community in the hills above Hebden Bridge, many of the names of the signatories were similar, so an official was dispatched to investigate. Having satisfied himself that all was in order, the official asked the petition organiser why almost everyone in the village had the same surname. "Because we don't yet have a bus service", came the unexpected reply.

Above: *The vehicles best remembered by many as the quintessence of Todmorden buses were the 30 all-Leyland PD2/1s bought in the post-World War II years. Here No.6 (HWY 33) dating from 1950, has just negotiated a hairpin bend, as it climbs out of the Worth Valley from Oxenhope to Cock Hill Moor on the Keighley to Hebden Bridge service in the 1960s.* Robert F. Mack

ACKNOWLEDGEMENTS

So many people have contributed to this publication, that it is not possible to mention them all individually. I am grateful to fellow enthusiasts with whom I have corresponded occasionally, including the late-Dennis O'Neill, regarded by many as the guru of Todmorden transport history, and fellow chartered accountant Mike Sutcliffe, whose extensive knowledge and expertise covers most aspects of Leyland (and especially Todmorden) buses.

I am particularly appreciative of the help given by Robert Priestley, of the Todmorden Antiquarian Society, and by Alan Earnshaw and his colleagues at Trans-Pennine Publishing. Thanks must also be expressed to the *Todmorden News & Advertiser*, Venture Publishing/TPC and the Oakwood Press for their permission to use quotations, to the staff of Calderdale Archives and Reference Library for their patient help and to Maurice Gordon, who cajoled me into embarking on the project.

The illustrations have been taken from either the slide collection of the Todmorden Antiquarian Society (those credited to TAS) or my own collection of photographs, slides, postcards and ephemera. The former was largely built up by Dennis O'Neill, while the latter has been built up over a lifetime by gift, by purchase at numerous fairs or via the internet, and from traders such as Photobus. The Roy Marshall photographs were acquired through East Pennine Transport Group, Frank Woolrych supplied pictures from the Alice Longstaff Gallery Collection, and John Uttley the one from the Jack Uttley Photo Library. It is inevitable that, in a book covering 100 years, many of the original photographers are no longer alive. Whilst every effort has been made to identify and contact the photographers and/or the current copyright holders, in a number of cases the relevant information has proved elusive, or in a few cases conflicting, and sincere apologies are offered for any unintentional breaches of etiquette.